# PILGRIMS and PURITANS

1620–1676

★ ★ *The Drama of* AMERICAN HISTORY ★ ★

# PILGRIMS
# and PURITANS

## 1620–1676

Christopher Collier
James Lincoln Collier

*BENCHMARK BOOKS*

MARSHALL CAVENDISH
NEW YORK

ACKNOWLEDGMENT: The authors wish to thank Harry S. Stout, John B. Madden Master of Berkeley College, Jonathan Edwards Professor of American Christianity, Yale University, for his careful reading of the text of this volume of The Drama of American History and his thoughtful and useful comments. The work has been much improved by Professor Stout's notes. The authors are deeply in his debt, but of course, assume full responsibility for the substance of the work, including any errors that may appear.

Photo research by James Lincoln Collier
Cover photo: © *Plimoth Plantation, Inc.*
PICTURE CREDITS: The photographs in this book are used by permission and through the courtesy of: © *Plimoth Plantation, Inc.*: 10, 28, 40, 46. *Corbis-Bettmann*: 15, 24, 26, 37 (top), 37 (bottom), 42, 72, 77, 82, 84. *Jamestown-Yorktown Educational Trust*: 18 (*detail*), 29. *Pilgrim Society*: 30, 58, 59, 60, 65, 66 (left), 66 (right), 67. © *Plimoth Plantation, Inc./Ted Curtin*: 31, 32, 33, 43, 49, 50, 53, 56, 57, 75, 78. © *Plimoth Plantation, Inc./Gary Andrashko*: 54, 55, 74.

AUTHORS' NOTE: The human beings who first peopled what we now call the Americas have traditionally been called *Indians*, because the first Europeans who landed in the Americas thought they had reached India. The term *Indians* is therefore not very accurate, and other terms have been used: *Amerinds*, and more recently, *Native Americans*. The Indians had no collective term for themselves. Today, most of them refer to themselves as Indians, and we will use that term here, while understanding that it is not very accurate.

Benchmark Books
Marshall Cavendish Corporation
99 White Plains Road
Tarrytown, New York 10591-9001

© 1998 Christopher Collier and James Lincoln Collier

Library of Congress Cataloging-in-Publication Data

Collier, Christopher, date
Pilgrims and Puritans, 1620–1676/
Christopher Collier and James Lincoln Collier.
p. cm. — (The drama of American history)
Includes bibliographical references and index.
Summary: Recounts the religious, political, and social history of the
Massachusetts Bay Colony, and its influence on our lives today.
ISBN 0-7614-0438-4 (lib. bdg.)
1. Pilgrims (New Plymouth Colony)—Juvenile literature. 2. Puritans—Massachusetts—
History—17th century—Juvenile literature. 3. Massachusetts—History—
New Plymouth, 1620-1691—Juvenile literature.
[1. Pilgrims (New Plymouth Colony) 2. Puritans. 3. Massachusetts—History—New Plymouth.
1620–1691.] I. Collier, James Lincoln, date. II. Title. III. Series: Collier, Christopher, date
Drama of American history.
F68.C693   1998                                    96-49382
974.4'8202—dc21                                    CIP
                                                    AC
Printed in the United States of America

1   3   5   6   4   2

# CONTENTS

PREFACE        7

CHAPTER I      Pilgrims and Puritans: The English Calvinists  9

CHAPTER II     The Pilgrims Come to a Desolated
                   Land and Mistake It for Eden  20

CHAPTER III    John Winthrop Leads Some Puritans Out of England  35

CHAPTER IV    The Puritans Establish Their Bible Commonwealth  48

CHAPTER V     Bible Commonwealths Spread Across New England  63

CHAPTER VI    The Indians Go to War to Stop the Puritan Invasion  70

CHAPTER VII   The Puritan Experiment Fails, But Leaves a
                   Mighty Legacy  80

BIBLIOGRAPHY  87

INDEX      90

# PREFACE

Over many years of both teaching and writing for students at all levels, from grammar school to graduate school, it has been borne in on us that many, if not most, American history textbooks suffer from trying to include everything of any moment in the history of the nation. Students become lost in a swamp of factual information, and as a consequence lose track of how those facts fit together, and why they are significant and relevant to the world today.

In this series, our effort has been to strip the vast amount of available detail down to a central core. Our aim is to draw in bold strokes, providing enough information, but no more than is necessary, to bring out the basic themes of the American story, and what they mean to us now. We believe that it is surely more important for students to grasp the underlying concepts and ideas that emerge from the movement of history, than to memorize an array of facts and figures.

The difference between this series and many standard texts lies in what has been left out. We are convinced that students will better remember the important themes if they are not buried under a heap of names, dates, and places.

In this sense, our primary goal is what might be called citizenship education. We think it is critically important for America as a nation and Americans as individuals to understand the origins and workings of the public institutions which are central to American society. We have asked ourselves again and again what is most important for citizens of our democracy to know so they can most effectively make the system work for themselves and the nation. For this reason, we have focused on political and institutional history, leaving social and cultural history less well developed.

This series is divided into volumes that move chronologically through the American story. Each is built around a single topic, such as the Pilgrims, the Constitutional Convention, or immigration. Each volume has been written so that it can stand alone, for students who wish to research a given topic. As a consequence, in many cases material from previous volumes is repeated, usually in abbreviated form, to set the topic in its historical context. That is to say, students of the Constitutional Convention must be given some idea of relations with England, and why the revolution was fought, even though the material was covered in detail in a previous volume. Readers should find that each volume tells an entire story that can be read with or without reference to other volumes.

Despite our belief that it is of the first importance to outline sharply basic concepts and generalizations, we have not neglected the great dramas of American history. The stories that will hold the attention of students are here, and we believe they will help the concepts they illustrate to stick in their minds. We think, for example, that knowing of Abraham Baldwin's brave and dramatic decision to vote with the small states at the Constitutional Convention will bring alive the Connecticut Compromise, out of which grew the American Senate.

Each of these volumes has been read by esteemed specialists in its particular topic; we have benefited from their comments.

# CHAPTER I

# Pilgrims and Puritans: The English Calvinists

They set out from Southampton, a thriving port city on the southern coast of England, in two sailing ships that today would seem foolishly small. Almost immediately one of the ships, called the *Speedwell*, began to spring leaks. They put in at Dartmouth for repairs, then started off again out into the vast Atlantic, two corks bobbing on an uncertain sea. They were well out into the ocean when once again the *Speedwell* began to leak, and threatened to sink. There was no choice, and the two ships turned back. They made land safely at Plymouth, a bustling port near the western tip of England.

Now as many of the *Speedwell* passengers as there was room for were transferred to the other ship, called the *Mayflower*, and it set off alone across the dangerous Atlantic, crowded with 101 passengers and the ship's crew. Week after week these Pilgrims traveled onward, men, women, and children (two babies were born aboard ship), along with such things as household furniture, tools, barrels of salted beef, casks of butter, and hogsheads of beer, which at the time was thought safer to drink than water. There were also some dogs on the ship, and probably pigs and chickens.

*The* Mayflower II, *a replica of the original* Mayflower, *as it appeared in 1957. At 180 tons, the* Mayflower *was larger than typical ships of the time. It was an excellent ship, and had seen many years of service hauling fish, timber, turpentine, and tar, mainly from Norway.*

Supplies of fresh food began to run short, and inevitably people grew sick. Scurvy, a common disease caused by a lack of vitamin C, grew rampant. Only one passenger died on shipboard, but by the end of the voyage many more were so ill that they would not survive the coming winter. They prayed; and finally, after almost eight weeks at sea, they saw the piece of land their maps called Cape Cod.

They sent out an expedition to see if there was any suitable place to settle in. The weather was so cold that as the explorers rowed for shore in their boat, the salt spray froze on their coats, glazing them over. They spent a night huddled around a fire, and all the next day searched the area. The next night they built a barricade of logs and brush, and once more huddled around the fire. Suddenly, as they were getting breakfast, they "heard a great and strange cry. 'Men, Indians, Indians,' someone shouted, and withal, their arrows came flying amongst them." The Pilgrims fired back, and some of the Indians fled. But one stood by a tree, speeding arrows toward them, until a musket shot ripped into the tree, flinging bits of wood and bark into his face. He gave "an extraordinary shriek," and fled.

Thus the Pilgrims were greeted in North America. They decided, after further explorations, that the sandy soil of Cape Cod was not promising for farming. They searched up the coast for a good place to settle. Finally, according to tradition, on December 21, 1620, they stepped out onto a piece of rock at a place that had already been named Plymouth by an enterprising explorer named John Smith, of the legend of Pocahontas, who had sailed up this coast a few years earlier. (For the story of Pocahontas see *The Paradox of Jamestown*, the second book of this series.) Historians today doubt the story of Plymouth Rock; but there is no question that at its location the Pilgrims began to build what would later be the most famous of all the early settlements in America, Plymouth Plantation.

Actually, there was already a small English colony on the American shores, founded in 1607 in Virginia. Its center was Jamestown, at first hardly more than a fort. The Virginia settlers had come—or been sent— to make a profit for themselves and their company back in England. They struggled at first, but by 1614 or so they had begun to cultivate tobacco, which they could sell very profitably in England and elsewhere in Europe. The Jamestown settlers established two institutions that proved to be of immense importance to what two and a half centuries later would become the United States. For one, they began to import black slaves from the Caribbean to help plant, hoe, and harvest the tobacco. At first a trickle, the stream of slaves grew to a flood, until slavery came to be a central institution in the South, and common enough in the North. The effects of slavery are with us today in the racial friction that has troubled America throughout its history.

*Jamestown, recreated to look as it did in the seventeenth century. The town was essentially a fort, well guarded against the possibility of Indian attack.*

There are in the United States a number of historic parks where early towns and villages have been carefully reconstructed, based on scrupulous research. Among the best-known are Williamsburg, Jamestown, and Plimouth Plantation, as the last was spelled in the early days. These historic parks often present reenactments of events and daily life of their times. Many of the pictures in this book are of the Jamestown and Plimouth Plantation parks. We should remember that the reenactments, while quite accurate in all details, use for the most part newly made clothing and tools. The originals would have been shabbier and perhaps patched, the tools more battered, plates and glasses chipped. Nonetheless, these reenactments can give us a very good picture of how life was lived in early colonial America.

A second institution developed in Virginia would also have profound effects on later Americans. The whole idea of a colony was new to the English. They had never really sat down and figured out how one should be governed. It took a long time for news from Virginia to reach London and for instructions to come back. It was clear that the colonists must be able to make some decisions on their own. Various schemes were tried, and out of the confusion there arose the House of Burgesses, made up of representatives elected by the villages of Virginia. This legislative body had only limited powers, but in a world where most people were ruled by monarchs with almost unfettered authority, the idea of this little legislature was very unusual. It was a first step toward self government in America. (Readers interested in more detail on the Virginia Colony will find it in *The Paradox of Jamestown*, the second book of this series.)

The Virginia settlers had come to make money for themselves and their financial backers. The people who came to New England arrived with quite different ideas in their heads. They wanted nothing less than to found a religious society in which the citizens would strive always to live in godly ways, dedicating themselves to God's service, and dwelling in peace and harmony with their fellow Christians. They were not merely carrying the old society to new shores; they intended to build something different. And the first of them were that little group who stepped ashore at Plymouth.

The legend of the *Mayflower* Pilgrims and the little town they built is one of the great stories in American history. In fact as things worked out, the Plymouth Colony proved to be less important to the American saga than legend makes it, for reasons that we shall look at in due course. But Plymouth was the starting point, and from such small beginnings do massive enterprises grow.

To understand why these hundred or so people made that desperate voyage, we have to know something about the situation in England in their day. It was a country in turmoil. For one thing, after the long and stable reign of Elizabeth I, there came a time of much quarreling among factions in government. In particular, the Parliaments of the seventeenth century were attempting to take power away from the kings, and the kings of course resisted. In time there would be open warfare between king and Parliament.

For another, England, like much of Europe, was in the midst of the long-term, but profoundly important, switch from a farming economy to "capitalism"—the system of trade and manufacturing in which most Americans, Europeans, and others elsewhere today live and work. In the days of the Pilgrims this switch was throwing a lot of people off the land and out of their cottages, to find jobs as best they could. Tens of thousands of English people were wandering country roads and city streets, looking for work—sleeping under hedges, begging and stealing when they could not find jobs.

For the Pilgrims, the most significant of the problems besetting England was the whole question of religion. At that time there were of course people everywhere, as there are in America today, who did not take religion very seriously. Nonetheless, for many if not most English people then, religion was a critically important matter. Adults lived much shorter lives than people do today, and about half the children died before reaching the age of ten. A concern for life after death in heaven or hell was very real. Thus they believed very strongly in their own ideas about God and their own ways of worshiping him. Small points were important, and people were frequently quite intolerant of other people's religious opinions.

For many centuries up to the 1500s, Roman Catholicism, headed by the pope in Rome, had been the

*Sir Walter Raleigh, a favorite of Elizabeth I, was instrumental in persuading his queen to begin the settlement of North America by the English. Raleigh's attempts to colonize Virginia did not succeed, but they opened the way for the settlement of Jamestown and, ultimately, New England. Here he is shown with his son.*

official religion almost everywhere in Europe. Virtually all Europeans were Roman Catholics. From time to time small groups with different ideas had tried to break away to form their own churches, but these efforts were invariably put down, frequently with a good deal of bloodshed and, often enough, torture.

By the early 1500s, new ideas were gaining some headway. Certain religious leaders, especially Martin Luther and John Calvin, were openly protesting against the Catholic Church. These Protestant ideas were complex and varied. To simplify a great deal, Luther, Calvin, and others believed that the Roman Catholic Church had gotten too rich, fat, and lazy. It seemed to them that many bishops, priests, abbots, and abbesses were too much concerned with the outward forms of religion at the expense of the inner spirit. The Protestants felt that Roman Catholic prelates spent too much on building huge cathedrals filled with gold and silver chalices and censers, too much on showy robes and jewelry, too much on their palaces and scores of servants. People like Luther and Calvin wanted to purify the church by eliminating these worldly activities.

In England the influence of John Calvin was especially strong. Many English people came to accept his ideas. This version of Puritanism, now called Calvinism, was taken up by a great many people.

Then, in 1534, Henry VIII, king of England, broke away from the Roman Catholic Church. He proclaimed that he, not the pope, would be head of what would be called the Anglican Church, or Church of England as it is usually called today. (Its American descendant is the Episcopal Church.) Henry broke with the Roman church for political rather than religious reasons. As a practical matter, since Henry VIII was not a Calvinist, the Anglican Church went along pretty much as the old Roman Catholic Church had done.

Not every English person agreed with Henry VIII's decision. Many of them still believed in Roman Catholicism and for some decades would try to "bring England back to Rome," as the phrase was. But this was now treason and could be punished by death. Most people accepted Henry's change, and very quickly patriotic English people came to see the Roman Catholic Church as the enemy of their nation.

By the late 1500s, the religious situation in England was exceedingly confused. The majority belonged to the official Anglican Church. Many Englishmen still clung to Roman Catholicism, but this group included numerous powerful noblemen. The Calvinists were a fairly large minority, but they were split into a number of factions, each with slightly different ideas about how people should live and God should be worshiped.

Through the years after Henry VIII's death England was beset by fierce religious battling as various groups struggled to get the upper hand. Many people from all groups were hung, burned at the stake, or beheaded for their religious beliefs.

We must understand that religion was a very serious matter for these people. That was particularly true of the Protestant Calvinists. If somebody lets a stone fall from his hand, you don't just *think* it will fall to the ground; you *know* it will. In the same way, these Puritans *knew* that there was a God, a heaven and a hell, a devil, witches, and that prayer worked. They were equally sure that everything on earth and in the heavens was created by God to glorify himself. The earth was God's, human beings were God's, and so was their labor and even their time. And God continued to rule the universe even to the details of every individual's life.

Several things followed from this idea. One was that the purpose of life was not to find happiness; it was to glorify God. This was done in two ways. One was to worship him through prayer, study of the Bible, and thinking and conversing about how he wanted you to live. The other was to serve God by serving his creatures, most importantly your fellow human beings. Furthermore, because a person's life was really God's, to be lazy or do less than your best at *anything* you did was simply sinful.

However, these Calvinists were not "puritanical" in the modern sense of the word. They believed that they could not do God's work without

*An engraving from 1594, showing European settlers building a boat in Panama.
The* Mayflower *was considerably larger than the boat being built here, but the
construction technique, using rough hand tools, was much the same.*

refreshing themselves from time to time. They enjoyed good food and
drink, dressed in bright colors, played games, and told stories. The point
was that these things were to be enjoyed in moderation. It was good to
enjoy a mug or two of beer, but it was bad to get drunk.

Underlying a lot of this Calvinist thinking was the concept of a
covenant with God—that is, an agreement or contract. God had made a
covenant with the biblical Abraham, promising salvation in return for

faith from Abraham's people, the Israelites. He made a second "covenant of redemption" with Jesus Christ, and as a consequence God offered the covenant of grace—that is, a chance to go to heaven instead of hell—to all who achieved faith in him. This idea of the covenant was thus familiar to the Calvinists and, as we shall see, they carried it over into their political life.

When we think about these Calvinist Puritans and Pilgrims, whose ways of thinking would have considerable influence on our lives today, we must try to imagine what it felt like to them to go around all day certain—or at least hoping—that they were doing God's work, and more than that, that they were building a new and better world. It must have been an exciting feeling to be part of such an endeavor.

# CHAPTER II

# The Pilgrims Come to a Desolated Land and Mistake It for Eden

Let us sum up the situation in England in the years just before 1600. Because of a long-term shift in the economy, there was a lot of unemployment and a good deal of unrest. The power struggle between Parliament and king, which would eventually lead to civil war, was keeping things in an unsettled state. Religious divisions, which sometimes also led to bloodshed, were adding to the confusion. Now we can begin to see why the Pilgrims were willing to make that desperate voyage across the Atlantic to build new lives in an untamed wilderness. Perhaps we can also see glimmerings of something even more important—that is, how the ideas of these early New England Calvinists have come to affect the ways Americans think about themselves, their jobs and families, their country. The seeds of much that we feel, think, and do as Americans were planted by the New England Calvinists.

Let us, then, go back to an earlier moment and see what happened to put those Pilgrims on the *Mayflower*.

Among the more extreme of the Calvinists were the Separatists. Most Protestants were basically trying to reform the established churches. The Separatists, however, reasoned that a church filled with people who were not serious about their religion was no church at all. Only a people deeply committed to God's commands could be called a true church. To the Separatists it was simply wrong to worship in the presence of people who were not as saintly as themselves, and they wanted to separate themselves from the official Anglican Church.

This was illegal. It did not much please the king to be told that his church was not a true church. While English kings could, and did, go along to some extent with ordinary Puritans, the Separatists were going too far, and the authorities did what they could do to break up Separatist congregations, sometimes putting their leaders in jail and even executing them.

At the beginning of the 1600s, there existed in a little town called Scrooby in the center of England one such Separatist group. Among its leaders was a man called William Brewster, born in 1567. His father had been in charge of a large estate owned by the Anglican Church in Scrooby and was somewhat better off than most of the farming people in the area. He sent William to Cambridge University. The university was at the time filled with debate over the religious controversies we have been looking at. Young Brewster became convinced of the rightness of the Calvinist beliefs. He was a very personable, cheerful, and well-spoken young man, and he got a position with a man who was important in the court of Queen Elizabeth, who ascended the throne in 1558. The position only lasted for four years, but the experience gave Brewster an understanding of how power and politics worked in the court.

The job over, he returned to Scrooby, where he joined the local Separatist group. Here he met a younger man, William Bradford. Bradford had been orphaned as a child and had grown up unhappily with relatives. Sickly as a youth, he grew into a strong, resourceful young man. Brewster took Bradford under his wing, almost as a son.

But pressure on the Separatists was growing. In 1593, Queen Elizabeth's archbishop of Canterbury had three of the Separatist leaders executed for their beliefs. These men had been with Brewster at Cambridge, and the warning had to be taken seriously.

The Scrooby group continued to meet in secret, but danger was everywhere, and finally, in 1607, some of the little group were arrested and imprisoned. Others fled from their houses and desperately sought aid and shelter from friends and family elsewhere. Now the Scrooby group began to think seriously of following the course taken by other Separatists before them—emigration from England.

It is no small thing for people to give up their homes, the towns and villages where they have spent their lives, and say good-bye to family perhaps forever. But they felt it was either flee or give up their religion, and they would not do that.

In 1608, they moved to Amsterdam, a city in Holland, a country that tolerated religious dissent. From Amsterdam they moved on to the town of Leyden, also in Holland. But there were problems. It was hard for these English immigrants to find good trades. They worked at weaving, baking, and printing, putting in long hours for low pay.

Much worse, these exiled Separatists were having difficulty controlling their children. Though Calvinist congregations existed in Holland, the Dutch were easygoing and liked to enjoy the simple pleasures of life: eating, drinking, cards, music. They tended to spend their Sundays lingering over a big meal rather than at worship. The young Separatists, like young people everywhere, found the relaxed Dutch attitude more attractive than the devout ways of their parents. Some joined the army; some went to sea with the busy Dutch merchant fleet. Others took "worse courses, tending to dissoluteness and the danger of their souls, to the great grief of their parents and dishonor of God," as one of their leaders later put it. The disloyalty of the young was a serious matter, for if the children did not follow in their parents' path, the godly community would soon die out.

Like most Europeans, these English Separatists were hearing about the explorations along the North American coast and the settlements at Jamestown, on Bermuda, and in the Caribbean. How much information they had we do not know, but Dutch merchant ships were sailing everywhere, and word of the New World colonies certainly got to the Separatists in Holland and England. They knew about the dangers of the Atlantic crossing, of rough conditions in the wilderness, of the threat of Indian arrows.

But it was clear to them that they would never be able to build their godly community in Holland. They would be able to do that only in some empty wilderness, where there would be no jolly Dutch way of life to lure away their children.

The obstacles confronting them were enormous. They were small in number, they had no money beyond what they earned for their daily livings, and their religion was hated by the English king, James I, who followed Elizabeth on the throne and reigned from 1603 to 1625. But they did have one thing: They *knew* that they had been chosen by God to found a community of the righteous. Their faith was absolute: If God had chosen them, he would open a path for them.

Over the years between 1617 and 1620, the Leyden Separatists worked up several plans for emigration and negotiated with various groups for financial backing. Eventually they made a deal with a somewhat foolhardy merchant named Thomas Weston, who was looking for colonists to settle some land he had rights to in the Virginia Colony. The Leyden people were a bit leery of the proposition, for the Virginia Colony was controlled by Anglicans, who might interfere with their wish to worship in their own way. But finally they accepted the proposal; it seemed their only chance.

In the end, only thirty-five of the Leyden community could, or would, go on this famous flight into the wilderness. Some were too old or too ill to go; others planned to come later. This was too small a number to found a colony. Weston therefore insisted that they take along a number of

*A painting by an unknown Dutch master, of the departure of the Pilgrims from Holland. The picture is imaginative, but it indicates the widespread interest in these early ventures into the wilderness of the New World.*

"strangers," people who were not of their religion, but who might have some useful skills. One of these was a short, fiery man named Miles Standish, a soldier practiced at warfare. Another was John Alden, a cooper—that is, a barrel maker—who went to oversee barrels containing beer and other supplies.

Alden intended to come back to London with the *Mayflower*. But according to the famous legend, he fell in love with another of the *Mayflower* passengers, the eighteen-year-old Priscilla Mullins. She must have been very attractive, for Standish eventually fell in love with her, too. Not knowing how Alden felt, Standish asked Alden to speak in his favor to Priscilla. As the legend has it, she responded, "Speak for yourself, John." He did, and they were married.

But that was later. In any case, the voyage of the *Mayflower* Pilgrims is one of the most famous immigrations in American history. It ended with the landfall on Cape Cod and the beginnings of New England.

And why, if these Pilgrims were bound for Virginia, did they land so far north? Historians are not sure. The Pilgrims themselves later suggested that it had been an accident. Since Plymouth is only a half degree north of the Hudson River, the northern limit of the Virginia bounds, this is perhaps the truth. It was convenient for the Pilgrims to stay there, however, in order to escape from the authority of the Virginia Colony, which favored the Anglican Church. Codfish, not tobacco, they assumed, would be their cash crop.

The change had momentous consequences for the development of English law and culture in America. The first of these appeared immediately. As soon as it was clear that the colony would be established outside of Virginia's borders, several of the strangers—the non-Separatists aboard—announced that they were no longer under any government and would do as they pleased once on land. Who precisely these rebels were we are not sure. It has been speculated that among them were two servants brought along by one of the strangers, Edward Dotey and Edward Leister, both hot-blooded young men who later on fought in a duel, for which they were tied together head to head and feet to feet as punishment.

Whatever the case, the Pilgrim leaders recognized that if people were allowed to go off on their own, rather than working together for the general good, the colony would not long survive. They drew up a document, which today we call the Mayflower Compact. In it the Pilgrims agreed that they would "covenant and combine ourselves together into a civil body politic, for our better ordering and preservation. And by virtue thereof do enact, constitute and frame such just and equal laws, ordinances, acts, constitutions and offices, from time to time, as shall be thought most meet and convenient for the general good of the colony; unto which we promise all due submission and obedience. . . ."

Most of the men signed it, and then elected their first governor, John Carver, a man in his fifties who had done some negotiating with the colony's financial backers.

The Mayflower Compact did not set up a government as such. It merely said that the signers could, and would, set up a government that they all agreed to obey. Nor was it a truly democratic document in the modern sense. As the Plymouth government worked out, the males, apparently including servants, voted for officers, who in turn ran things as they thought they ought to.

Nonetheless, it was a major step forward. Today the idea of a small group of this kind organizing itself in this way is commonplace. In those days it was not. In the seventeenth century all people saw themselves as living in a hierarchical society, in which everybody had a specific place on the social and

*Edward Winslow, a key figure in the Plymouth Colony and long its governor. This portrait was painted in 1651 by an unknown artist, at a time when the New England colonies were well established.*

political ladder. People were expected to be obedient to the command of those above them: wives to their husbands, children to their fathers, apprentices to their masters, farmers to their lords, and everybody to the king. Even in England, which was somewhat more open than most nations, only a small percentage of people could vote on anything at all. In small municipalities and some church organizations elections were held, but in general, decisions affecting huge numbers were settled by those who had acquired the right to do so by birth, purchase, or some high official's favor.

Like most English people, the *Mayflower* Pilgrims accepted the idea of obedience to authority. The Mayflower Compact, however, introduced to America the idea of a written agreement among the people voluntarily to establish and obey a government. It was a political compact paralleling the theological compact with God written down in the Bible. In the 1680s, this idea would become central to the theory of Social Contract made famous by John Locke and adopted nearly a century after Locke's time as the official philosophy of the United States in the Declaration of Independence.

But despite this hopeful first step, the Pilgrims were faced with bleak prospects. Many of them were very sick from the long voyage. Winter was on them and it snowed several times before they left Cape Cod and moved to Plymouth. Food was obviously going to be in short supply.

Nonetheless, they buckled down. The place they had chosen to build their little settlement was not woods, but cleared land. Indeed, a great deal of the eastern seaboard of North America had been cleared by Indians to make fields for corn, squash, beans, and other crops. The gardens that lay before the Pilgrims at Plymouth were now abandoned.

The human beings who first peopled what we now call the America have traditionally been called Indians, because the first Europeans who landed in the Americas thought they had reached India. The term *Indians* is therefore not very accurate, and other terms have been used: *Amerinds,* and more recently, *Native Americans*. The Indians had no term for themselves, as they thought they were all the human beings that there were. Today most of them refer to themselves as Indians, and we will use that term here, while understanding that it is not very accurate. (For a discussion of Indian lifestyles see *Clash of Cultures*, the first book of this series.)

The story of why the English settlers found fields ready-made for their corn is one of the greatest tragedies of the land. The Indians of the Americas had been isolated from the rest of the world's peoples for at least twenty thousand years. They had never been exposed to many diseases that were common in Europe. People in a region generally build up

*A Plimouth Plantation reenactment of Indians in typical costumes of the time. Many of the people used in these reenactments are descendants of New England Indian tribes.*

*An Indian celt, or ax head, five inches by two inches. It is well over four hundred years old and was found in Virginia. The Indians were extremely skilled at making fine tools from stone, as this celt shows.*

a certain amount of immunity to local diseases. For example, while many thousands of Europeans died of smallpox every year, most of those who caught the disease got over it, although they might be scarred by it. But the Indians had not been exposed to such diseases. Through the 1500s and into the 1600s, European explorers, conquerors, fishermen, and finally settlers, brought to America diseases such as measles, smallpox, the plague. A disease like measles, no longer lethal, was deadly to the Indians, who had not acquired any immunity to it. Frequently when a disease hit an area, it would in a few weeks wipe out village after village, leaving only a handful of people where hundreds had lived.

Thus the English settlers often found themselves moving into land depleted of Indians, with fields already cleared. If not for the diseases, the Pilgrims would have been coming into land filled with Indians, who would certainly not have wanted to move over to make room for these interlopers. It is likely that even before they left England, the Pilgrims had been aware of the epidemics that were emptying the land of the Indians. They would take this as a sign that God was clearing the land for them.

It was, in any case, a great advantage for the Pilgrims. They set about building little houses, and gradually moved off the *Mayflower* onto land. But their troubles were just beginning. Week after week they watched

*This cradle was used by Peregrine White, the first English child to be born in New England. His mother was pregnant when the* Mayflower *set sail, and they brought with them the cradle. Peregrine was actually born on the* Mayflower *after it had anchored off Plymouth in 1620. He lived to 1703, a time when New England was a thriving area.*

their fellows die; before the first year was over, half of the *Mayflower* passengers would be dead.

Supplying themselves with just the barest minimum of fresh food was a problem. The Pilgrims would not be able to plant corn until spring, and not until midsummer would they be able to eat it. But there were deer in the woods, fowl in the marshes around the bay, and the Pilgrims struggled on.

Then there were the Indians. For weeks after the settlers started building their little houses, they saw smoke from Indian fires, even occasionally spotted an Indian in the distance. But it was like whispers in the dark, for there was no contact.

Then one day there strode into camp a tall, virtually naked Indian who introduced himself in English as Samoset. The Pilgrims exchanged gifts with Samoset, and not long afterward he brought in another Indian, yet one more figure in the Pilgrim legend. This was Squanto. He had been captured by explorers and been taken to England, where he learned English. Eventually he made his way back to America. Here he discovered that his people had been wiped out by an epidemic.

In the Plymouth legend Squanto has often been seen as the man who saved the Pilgrims by showing them how to plant corn. And part of this is true. But Squanto had his own schemes. He was essentially a man without a tribe, and he hoped that if he got the backing of English muskets he could make himself a power among the local chiefs. It is one of the great tragedies of the Indians that they were more often interested in settling old grudges than in dealing with the intruding English settlers. As a result

*A reenactment of an Indian showing a Pilgrim how to plant corn. Squanto is reputed to have taught the newcomers to set a fish in each hill, to supply fertilizer as the corn seeds grew.*

*When the Pilgrims first arrived in New England, they sent some of the men out in a small boat, or shallop, to explore the country to find the best place to build their settlement. This reconstruction shows such a shallop, and men and women in typical clothes of the time.*

they often made alliances with the English against other Indian tribes. Squanto was following this old Indian custom.

He arranged a meeting with a powerful chief, Massasoit, whose followers had until recently dominated that corner of New England, but who was now so weakened by disease that they had to pay tribute to the Narragansett. Massasoit and the Pilgrims made a treaty of peace between them, which said simply that neither side would do the other any harm, and both would aid the other if attacked—which would of course bring English muskets in against Massasoit's Indian enemies if necessary. The treaty of peace held firm for forty years, until the death of Massasoit. With its signing, a great fear was lifted from the Pilgrims' hearts.

Finally spring came, bringing warm weather. The *Mayflower*, which had stayed through the winter to support the settlers, sailed for home in April. With Squanto's help the Pilgrims got their corn in. Slowly the death toll dropped, but not before Governor Carver, almost sixty, died of sunstroke in the fields. He was replaced by William Bradford, a vigorous man of thirty-two. Bradford was smart, energetic, and practical. With the help of Standish and others, such as Isaac Allerton and Edward Winslow, Bradford provided the Pilgrims with the strong leadership they needed.

That fall, with the harvest, the Pilgrims held that famous first Thanksgiving. They invited Massasoit. He brought with him ninety braves, far more than the Pilgrims had counted on. But the Indians went out and killed five

*A reenactment of the first Thanksgiving, which took place in the fall of 1621. The Pilgrims invited Massasoit, who turned up with ninety hungry braves. The Indians quickly went out and shot deer and other game, so there was plenty for all. The celebration went on for three days, with sports and games, as well as plenty of food.*

deer, and they all settled down for three days of playing games and feasting on venison, goose, duck, shellfish, corn bread, and wild plums, and, according to Governor Bradford, "a great store of turkeys." Thanksgiving symbolized for all of them that, however many problems lay ahead, the worst was over. It also held out the false hope that Indians and Europeans could live in peace in America. Tragically, as we shall see, that was not to be. Soon after Thanksgiving a ship called *Fortune* arrived with more Pilgrims. Other ships followed, and the little Pilgrim colony began to spread through the area around Plymouth.

But ironically, even as the Plymouth Colony was getting on its feet, there were about to take place in England a series of events that would see the little commonwealth overshadowed by a mighty neighbor. The main event in this era of American history would take place next door.

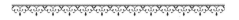

# CHAPTER III

# John Winthrop Leads
# Some Puritans Out of England

The Pilgrims, the *Mayflower*, Plymouth Rock, Sqaunto, and people such as Governor Bradford, the fiery warrior Miles Standish, and the lovers John Alden and Priscilla Mullins are at the core of one of the great legends in American history. But in fact the Massachusetts Bay Colony, which grew up a few years later some thirty miles to the north, had a far more profound effect on the development of New England and the future of the United States than did the little clutch of towns which extended only from Narragansett Bay to Hingham just south of Boston including Cape Cod. People like John White, John Cotton, and Thomas Dudley are certainly not nearly as well known as Bradford and Standish, and the Massachusetts towns of Sudbury and Charlestown are almost unknown to millions of Americans who know all about Plymouth. Yet Massachusetts rather than Plymouth played the dominant role in the story of this era of American history.

As we have seen, England in the years around 1600 was in turmoil, afflicted by warring factions in politics and religion that at times led to bloodshed. By the 1620s, when the Pilgrim colony at Plymouth was staggering to its feet, matters were getting worse. In 1625, a new king,

Charles I, came to the throne of England. He was autocratic and strongly anti-Puritan. He gave much power to William Laud, Bishop of London, who ground down hard on the Calvinists, and he heated up the battle with Parliament. It seemed to many English people that the country was headed for a collapse, and indeed in time a bloody war between Charles and Parliament would break out.

Not surprisingly, the idea of emigrating to the New World was being widely discussed in England by rich and poor alike. Many farm laborers and household servants felt there was no future for them in England, where they would spend their lives working for other people for tiny wages. Better to take a chance on the wilderness, the Indians, the dangerous Atlantic crossing, than to stay in a nation about to fall to pieces.

The English Puritans, or Calvinists as it is best to call them, had an even better reason for leaving than most people: The pressure on them to give up their religious beliefs was becoming intolerable.

There were a number of places to immigrate to. Tolerant Holland was one such place, but elsewhere in Europe war was raging. By the mid-1620s, North America was beginning to seem like a realistic possibility. The Virginia Colony around Jamestown was spreading, and earning a lot of money for the tobacco growers. The little band of Pilgrims was doing well. Dotted here and there along the coast, particularly in what are now Massachusetts and Maine, a few tiny fishing stations were clinging to the rocky shore. One of these settlements was already infamous. It was led by a lively rogue named Thomas Morton, who drank and caroused with Indian women, "dancing and frisking together like so many fairies or furies." This "godlessness" annoyed the Pilgrims, and they sent Miles Standish, whom Morton referred to as "Captain Shrimp, Quondam drummer," to stop the frisking.

We must understand that Protestantism, in general, was an *intellectual* movement. It was based on the work of religious philosophers such as John Calvin, who was especially influential in England and was the

Martin Luther was one of the first to break with the Roman Catholic Church and create the Reformation, which led to Protestantism and, eventually, the Puritanism of the early New England settlers. This portrait is by his celebrated contemporary, Lucas Cranach the elder.

The French theologian John Calvin was particularly influential among English Puritans, so much so that we frequently refer to the religion of the early New Englanders as Calvinism. This portrait is by the famous German painter Hans Holbein.

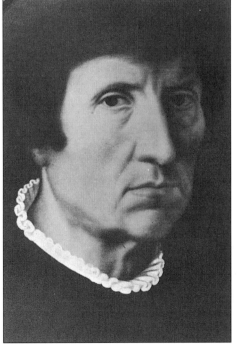

author of justly famous religious writings. The Puritans believed that you could only know what God wanted by a very close reading of his Word in the Bible. Their ministers and some of the best educated laymen studied the Bible in its original languages—Greek, Hebrew, and Aramaic—and they wrestled over hundreds of fine points of interpretation. Scholars at Cambridge University were particularly prone to this sort of religious debate, and it is not surprising that the area around the university produced a lot of Puritan ministers and other leaders.

But despite Morton's frisky encampment and the other small villages along the New England coast, most of the land thereabouts was unsettled by Europeans. Might it not be possible for Puritans to build in America a holy society entirely devoted to God?

This was a great vision. If they could build a godly society, they might set an example that the rest of the world could follow. They could change the world. A mighty idea, all right; and we can imagine how exhilarated it must have made them feel as they contemplated it. But could they do it?

If they were to make their vision real, it would have to be in some place that was not already populated, where they would be free to set up things as they liked. Massachusetts was the obvious choice; colonies were succeeding there and, more importantly, the example of Plymouth showed that a Calvinist community could exist there.

The Calvinist Puritans who would found the Massachusetts Bay Colony were somewhat different in their outlook from the Plymouth people. For one thing, the Pilgrims had never been much concerned about whether anyone followed their example—they simply wanted to be free to set up their own type of religious community. For another, although there were some educated people among the Pilgrims such as William Brewster, back in England most of them had been plain people—farmers and craftsmen of various kinds and their wives.

The people who were now looking toward New England with this great vision in mind were different. They came from everywhere in England, but they were particularly thick in the area to the northeast of London, known as East Anglia, around the cities of Norwich, Lincoln, and Cambridge. The presence there of Cambridge University was important. Perforce, they tended to be well-to-do. While it was possible for poor boys to study at a university on scholarship, inevitably the bulk of students at a place like Cambridge came from well-off families—the squires and lower nobility who made up the bulk of the English upper class. Of course among the Puritans most were plain people: farmers and craftsmen of various kinds. But an unusual proportion of them were gentlemen with good educations. The effect of this fact on America would be profound.

The Puritans looking toward America were not joined in a single organization. Although individual groups of Puritans were pretty well aware of what other groups were thinking and doing, they were scattered. And various of them were working separately toward the American venture.

The first Puritan leader to make headway was John White, a minister at Dorchester in the southwestern part of England, where ships routinely fitted out for the trip across the Atlantic. He was a brilliant speaker, who could "wind up" his parishioners "to what height he pleased on important occasions." As early as 1623 White and a group of gentlemen from the Devon area around Dorchester formed a company to send ships out to fish in the Atlantic and trade with the Indians. By 1624 there existed a tiny settlement on Cape Ann at what is now Gloucester, north of Boston. The settlers were supposed to catch fish, dry it, and keep it until ships came in the spring to take it home, meanwhile growing their own food. The scheme failed; the fishermen refused to do the landsman's hard labor of farming, and the farmers were poor fishers.

But White persuaded the leader of the group, Roger Conant, to stay on in hopes that the business could be revived somehow. Conant talked

*A reenactment of an early church service. In wintertime these churches were cold, and the services could last for hours, so people bundled up. The man in black in the front row has ammunition dangling from his belt: These early New Englanders went to church armed.*

many of the settlers into staying, and in 1626 they moved to a place called Salem, about twenty miles north of Boston.

Back in England, in 1628, White brought in some London investors and moved the company's headquarters there. Most of these investors were in fact Puritans, as was White. Somehow White managed to get a grant for a huge tract of land in New England; we are not sure how. The new company was called *The New England Company for a Plantation in Massachusetts Bay*, now generally known as the Massachusetts Bay Company. White and his partners sent over a man named John Endecott to take on the leadership of the colony. They gave Endecott "strongly puritanical instructions," and he sailed in June 1628. The next spring several more ships went out carrying passengers to Massachusetts Bay.

There was no doubt that this was to be a religious colony. No fewer than four ministers were sent over to tend to the souls of the colonists. At one point some young men arrived from England whom Endecott thought not sufficiently religious. He sent them right back to England, "rather than keep them to infect or be an occasion of scandal unto others." He also put an end to Thomas Morton's merry community, cutting down the maypole around which Morton's men and their Indian girlfriends used to frisk.

Although John White was among the first to actively promote a religious colony in New England (of course after the Pilgrims), a more important figure—indeed critically important—was a man named John Winthrop. He was an exceptional man, as were many of the Massachusetts Bay colonists. He was born on an estate called Groton Manor, which was owned by his father. It had a great house and a huge barn with a thatched roof; it was surrounded by fields and meadows where cattle grazed and wheat, rye, and other crops grew. Not surprisingly, the estate lay in Suffolk, one of the East Anglia counties where so many Puritans lived.

Winthrop grew up in this pretty English countryside in a house full of servants—not pampered, surely, but fortunate. At fifteen he was sent to Cambridge University. He was homesick at first, but stayed for two years. Shortly after he came home his father arranged for him to marry the daughter of another wealthy landowner, who lived nearby; such arranged marriages were common at that time. More important for American history, he also became deeply interested in the Puritan ideas that were gathering followers. One historian says that to John Winthrop Puritanism meant "the problem of living in this world without taking his mind off God." That was, indeed, the great Puritan dilemma: How do you live a

*John Winthrop gave up a large estate in England to come to New England to establish a religious community. He was elected governor before the colonists sailed from England, and was for a long time a powerful force in the community.*

godly life in a corrupt world? For a while he considered becoming a minister.

Winthrop liked to enjoy himself. He liked good food and drink, he liked hunting, he liked smoking his pipe. But over time he managed to get control over his great love of fun. Like most Puritans, he was not striving to eliminate good times from his life altogether, but he realized that he sometimes ate too much, played too much, and he knew he should aim for moderation. His life should be at the service of God, and he should have only such recreation as he needed to keep fresh in mind and body.

During his early adulthood Winthrop was occupied by managing his estates. For a period he studied law in London, for a squire like Winthrop had to act as a judge in local matters. But most importantly, he was getting to know other wealthy, educated men like himself who were Puritans, among them John White, who in a pamphlet said, "Who knows but that God that provided [America] to be a refuge for many whom he means to save out of the general calamity, and seeing the church hath no place left to fly into but the wilderness, what better work can there be,

*We often think of the Puritans as hating good times, good food and drink, but in fact they believed that it was necessary for them to enjoy themselves from time to time to be fresh for the work of God. They made rich pies, plucked wild grapes from vines in the woods, took shellfish from the sea, and made cheese from the milk of cows and goats. They ate a great deal of meat, for vegetables and fruit were scarce in the winter. The dishes here were prepared at Plimouth Plantation from early recipes.*

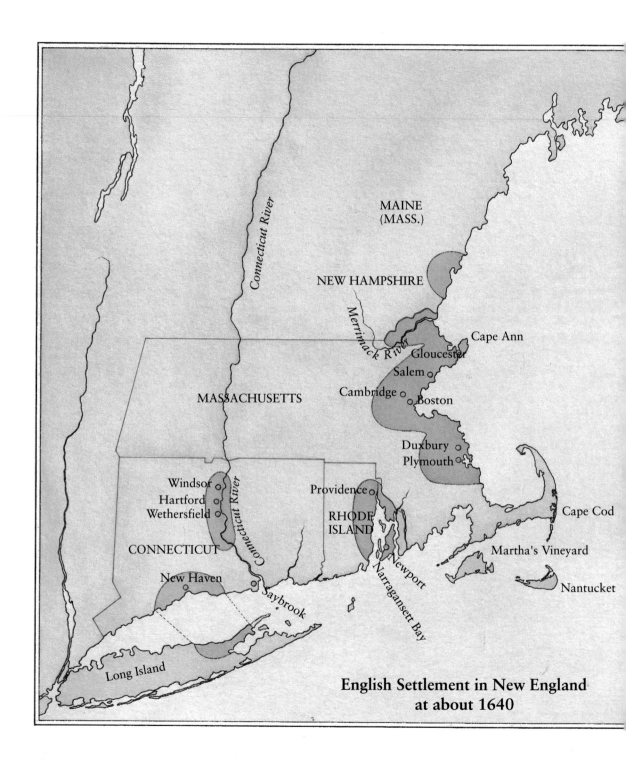

MAINE
(MASS.)

NEW HAMPSHIRE

*Merrimack River*

*Connecticut River*

MASSACHUSETTS

Cape Ann

Gloucester

Salem

Cambridge

Boston

Duxbury

Plymouth

Cape Cod

Windsor

Hartford

Wethersfield

*Connecticut River*

Providence

RHODE
ISLAND

Martha's Vineyard

Nantucket

CONNECTICUT

New Haven

Saybrook

Newport

*Narragansett Bay*

Long Island

**English Settlement in New England
at about 1640**

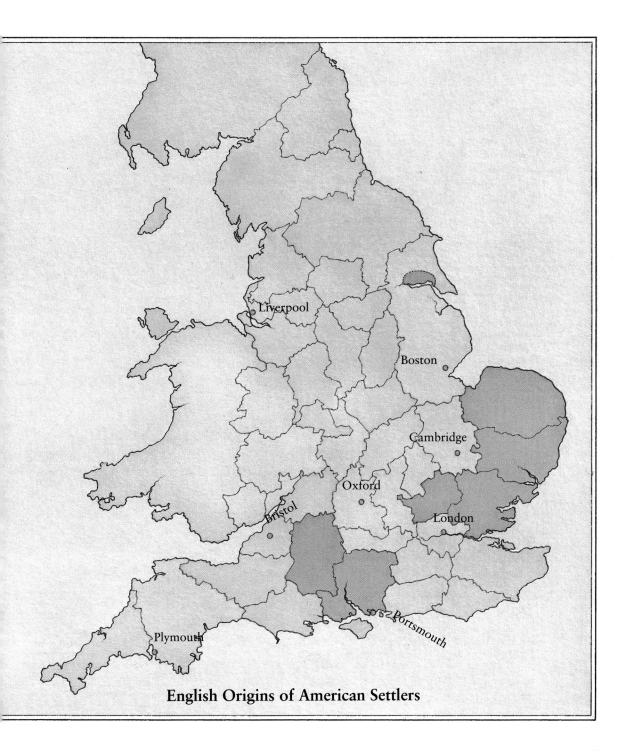

**English Origins of American Settlers**

*A reenactment at Plimouth Plantation of a hearty dinner, typical of the time.*

than to go and provide tabernacles and food for her [for when] she comes thither." Winthrop came to be persuaded by this line of thought. "My dear wife," he wrote about England, "I am verily persuaded God will bring some heavy affliction upon this land, and speedily. . . ." Winthrop was not alone: this was how many Puritans felt. England was done for, and they might as well get out while there was still a place to flee to.

Still, it was a great sacrifice. Winthrop would be leaving a very comfortable existence in a great house, with servants, a good deal of money, and as much work as he chose to do. In exchange he would live in an untamed wilderness, in a rough cottage, where death from disease was frequent and the Indians were a constant danger. But it was the choice he made. For in the end, the idea that he was about to embark on a great undertaking was a powerful attraction. So in March 1630 Winthrop sailed out of England as leader of an effort to do nothing less than build a religious society devoted to the glory of God and the peace of humankind. Could such a thing succeed?

If such a thing could, this might be the one. This errand into the wilderness was large, carefully planned, and well financed. It went in a fleet of no less than eleven ships carrying seven hundred passengers, forty cows, sixty horses, many goats, and a great collection of supplies and equipment. Indeed, the many whole families who came on this voyage showed that this was not an expedition of conquest and exploration as had been earlier efforts in Virginia and South and Central America. This was, rather, a religious movement and a social experiment. Moreover this was no small-scale effort like the Pilgrim venture, setting off in leaking ships with inadequate supplies at the wrong time of year. Among other things, the Winthrop group left early enough in the year to get a crop in the ground that spring. Their voyage would prove to be one of the most important sailings to America of all time.

# CHAPTER IV

# The Puritans Establish
# Their Bible Commonwealth

The huge immigrant fleet under John Winthrop arrived in Salem in June. The leaders quickly decided that the location was not good and traveled on to another settlement called Charlestown, which the Salem people had already established. But Charlestown proved to have an inadequate water supply, and some of the new arrivals, including Winthrop, moved on to a nearby peninsula known as Shawmut, where they began scratching together a village they called Boston, after a town in southern Lincolnshire where so many of the Puritans had lived.

The arrival of Winthrop, his seven hundred fellows, and their livestock and supplies changed the whole structure of the New England colonies. Because of its size, the new group instantly dominated the older settlements. The Massachusetts Bay people remained on reasonably good terms with the Pilgrims in their little villages around Plymouth, although the Pilgrims tended to keep their distance. But Salem and the other small communities along the coast were swallowed up in the Bay Colony. (Among others, Thomas Morton once more turned up and started frisking with the Indians again. Winthrop had him captured and sent back to England, where he began a campaign of complaints against the Bay Colony.)

Now Winthrop and his associates, among them Deputy Governor Thomas Dudley, the minister John Cotton, John Endecott, Richard Mather, and some others, began to create their new society, the godly "city on a hill." This was an extremely unusual, not to say daunting, task. Most societies evolve slowly, changing as conditions change. It is very rare for human beings to create their own society from scratch. Of course the Puritans did not abandon the English ways of living. They wanted to make changes in worship and improve the way in which people behaved. But they had no problems with a lot of the old English lifestyle.

For example, in England most people lived in little village clusters of thatched houses, with a church, a central common or green for grazing livestock, an inn, a well, all surrounded by fields and meadows which

*In English villages, houses were clustered around a church, a tavern, a store, and a common where the villagers could graze their family cows. The first New Englanders built their villages on the English model, as in this picture of Plimouth Plantation.*

*Early New England houses were generally made of overlapping clapboards nailed over a frame of heavy timbers. Roofs were thatched with straw in such a way that they kept out rain and snow. Paint was not available, so the houses went unpainted.*

were farmed either as compact parcels or in sections, with ploughing, planting, and harvesting organized on a community basis. The Massachusetts settlers' farming methods were the ones they knew at home, except that corn, not rye or wheat, was the main crop. They cooked in much the same way, and after they had brought over apple trees, they drank the same sort of cider and dressed much as they had at home.

But in some very basic matters they were determined to do things differently in New England. And here lay some very real dangers. Colonists venturing into the New World could not simply go out there and settle themselves in. Most of the land was claimed by one or more European powers (who ignored the fact that the Indians already occupied the land). A group of colonists had to get some kind of authorization in the form of a charter or patent in order to take over a piece of land. For English settlers this was arranged by the king or somebody to whom the king had already granted it.

But at the time that Winthrop sailed, nobody had carefully thought through the whole question of how these colonies should be governed. The king assumed that colonists were English subjects, who would therefore be at his command, but who would also have the rights traditionally given to English people.

Nonetheless, as we have seen, in Virginia the governor had had to authorize an elected House of Burgesses, providing greater self government than was the practice back in England. And in truth, the Massachusetts Bay leaders expected to have a fairly free hand to set up their colony as it suited them. It could hardly be otherwise, if they were to establish a godly community in New England. Winthrop, in a famous speech called "A Model of Christian Charity," said flatly that they were going into the wilderness

> ". . . to do justly, to love mercy, to walk humbly with our God. For this end we must be knit together in this work as one man; we must entertain each other in brotherly affection; we must be willing to abridge ourselves of our superfluities for the supply of others' necessities . . . rejoice together, mourn together, labor and suffer together always having before our eyes our commission and community in the work. . . . For we must consider that we shall be as a city upon a hill, the eyes of all people are upon us. . . ."

If they wished to build this city on a hill, they could hardly let the king tell them what to do. Among other things, the king of England was head of the Anglican Church, the very one that the Puritans were attempting to "purify." In theory the Puritans insisted that they were all good Anglicans, who just wanted to make certain changes in the way they worshiped. But in truth they really were out to erect a new religious system that in many respects went directly against the theology and practices of the Anglican Church the king was head of.

The Virginia colonists had their disputes with the king and his government from time to time—indeed at one point there was an actual rebellion in Virginia. But they were not reformers, not idealists. On the whole, the Virginians saw themselves as loyal subjects of the king and generally accepted the British system along with its official Anglican Church.

The Massachusetts Bay colonists *were* both reformers and idealists. Whatever they might say and indeed honestly believe about their loyalty to the king, in practice they were opposed to the British ecclesiastical system in a good many ways. We remember that Winthrop, White, and many of the rest believed that England was about to be hit by a "general calamity," "some heavy affliction" visited upon them by God. Clearly they must do things differently in the New World; and that would not necessarily please the king.

One thing that definitely would not please him was the Bay Colony's intention to follow God's word, as it came through the Bible, not the rules handed down from London. Their society must be built on service to God and love of one another, not on loyalty to king and country. Lying behind this idea was the concept of *limited government*. That is to say, the government could not do anything it wanted, but was limited by God's laws. This, of course, is in direct opposition to the idea of the divine right of kings, an idea that James I and later Charles I were trying to revive in England. This idea of limited government would in time become basic to the United States, where governments are limited by the Constitution, which says what our officials can and cannot do.

*Although the Pilgrims were generally on good terms with the Indians, there was among them a sense of danger. They usually were armed when they went any distance from the village.*

Thus, whatever the king thought, and whatever the Bay colonists said in public, in their hearts they intended to do what they felt they must do to establish their godly community. And they understood the political realities involved in this; so in one very bold act, they brought their charter to America. The charters for all other colonies had stayed in London. Winthrop took this one to America. With the charter in Massachusetts, no one in England (except, of course, in theory, the king) could tell them how to run their colony.

We should understand that these Puritan colonists had no intention of establishing a democracy in our sense of the word. Like most people everywhere, the Bay colonists accepted the idea that some were leaders and some followers and that was unlikely to change. The leaders interpreted the Bible, and individual rights were always limited by God's rules as they saw them.

*Typically, women raised vegetables in gardens near their houses. They also usually had charge of chickens, milked the family cow, and saw to the making of cheese and butter.*

Nonetheless, right from the beginning bits and pieces of self-government began to creep in. As originally set up in the Massachusetts Bay charter, the investors would choose a group from among themselves to pass basic laws. However, the "generality"—a term that turned out to be much too vague—would elect a governor, deputy governor, and a council of assistants to advise the governor.

Very quickly after landing, the government opened itself up. Winthrop and his council decided that all of the "freemen" of the colony could vote every year for the assistants, who in turn would elect a governor. A few years later they said that all male adults who were not servants could be considered freemen. There was one stipulation: A freeman had to be a church member, which meant not simply going to church regularly, but proving you were deeply religious and had heard God's voice or experienced his presence in some way.

Why Winthrop and the other leaders voluntarily gave up so much power we do not know for sure. They were undoubtedly impelled to do so in part by their own ideas. Weren't they supposed to show love for their fellows? What better way to show this love than to trust them with some power? And of course, as Winthrop knew, it is always easier to get people to follow their leaders if they have a hand in picking them. Gradually, bit by bit, the suffrage was widened. Soon freemen were vot-

*Large-scale farming for hay, wheat, corn, and similar crops was done on individual plots of land outside the village. As the New England population grew, farm plots were established farther and farther from the villages. In time, people with distant plots built houses near them, and eventually new villages grew up.*

*A typical homestead. The garden plot behind the house was fenced in to protect the vegetables from roaming cows and sheep. The animals of the English settlers often roved into Indian cornfields, and they were a constant source of friction between the Indians and the settlers.*

ing for the governor directly and electing representatives from their towns to join the assistants in making laws.

These steps in the direction of what centuries later would become American-style democracy grew in part out of the fact that the Puritans were used to setting up their own churches. They believed that any group, however small, that could agree on religious principles and a plan of worship, was qualified to establish a church. They had done this secretly in England many times. They continued to do it in New England, and they applied the same principle when it came to setting up their towns and villages. All that was needed was for the people involved to get together, work out covenants that they would all hold to, and elect their officers. These covenants were not like contracts between two parties, each trying to serve his own interest, however. They were voluntary agreements by which all members of the group gave up certain rights and privileges so that they could live together in peace and harmony under God's ordinances. The group, be it a church or a town, did not have to look anywhere for guidance other than in the Bible.

The covenant theory gave rise to the principle of congregationalism. In most western religions there is, even today, a central authority: for Roman Catholics the pope in the Vatican, for the Church of England the archbishop of Canterbury, for Presbyterians a synod or council of ministers and elders called a presbytery.

*Rolls and bread were baked in ovens heated with wood and were scooped out with large wooden paddles.*

The congregational idea, then and today, is that each congregation is the sole master of its own house, not under the sway of a higher religious authority. Thus, although the Puritans were not democrats in our modern sense, there was in practice a lot of self-determination involved in their way of governing.

But this does not mean that Puritans of the Massachusetts Bay Colony believed in religious freedom. Far from it; the opposite was true. The Puritans had come to New England with a carefully worked out and well-established set of beliefs and system of worship. They had struggled long and hard at interpreting the Bible, and they were certain they had come up with the truth. They had no intention of permitting people to preach ideas about God and religion that differed from theirs, for wrong theories would corrupt the whole community and condemn everyone to eternal hell.

One person to find this out, to his sorrow, was a man named Roger Williams. He was, like most Puritans, deeply religious. He also had a brilliant mind and

*This sampler was made by Laura Standish, daughter of the renowned Miles Standish. She made it when she was a teenager. It is the oldest-known sampler made in America.*

*A large chair that belonged to Miles Standish.*

as a youngster had attracted the attention of the great legal thinker Sir Edward Coke, who saw to it that Williams was educated at Cambridge, where so many of the Puritan leaders got their schooling. He had, moreover, quite an attractive personality. In 1631, he came to New England, drawn by the great events happening there. He was at first welcomed. But quickly it became clear that Roger Williams was pushing the logic of Calvinism a step further than Winthrop and his associates had taken it. Like the Plymouth Pilgrims, he was basically a Separatist who felt that anyone who wished to be free of sin had to make a clean break with the impure Anglican Church. In fact, Winthrop and the Bay colonists had pretty much separated themselves from the Anglican Church. But they were afraid to admit it, for fear they might get into some kind of trouble with the king, such as the revocation of their charter. They did not want Williams raising the issue. When it became clear to him he was no longer welcome in Massachusetts Bay, he and his wife moved down to Plymouth, where his Separatist opinions would be more acceptable.

When he got there he discovered that clergymen from the churches in the little towns around Plymouth had gotten into the habit of meeting occasionally to consult on various things. To Williams this seemed like a step away from congregationalism—that is, in the direction of creating a board of some kind that might have power over the individual congregations. He criticized this practice. To make matters worse, he announced that the king had had no right to give Massachusetts to the Puritans, because it had belonged to the Indians. On one point after another Williams came into conflict not only with the Plymouth Pilgrims, but with the Bay Colony to the north, too. The religious leaders there tried to persuade Williams that his opinions were wrong, but he was stubborn and went on preaching his dangerous views.

Finally the authorities lost patience and ordered Williams deported to England. The good-hearted Governor Winthrop realized that Williams would be in serious trouble with the king if he went back to England. He warned Williams that he was about to be arrested. On Winthrop's advice Williams fled south to what is now Rhode Island. He eventually hauled up on an estuary in Narragansett Bay, where he purchased land from the Indians and founded what would become

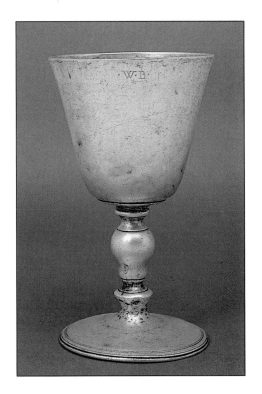

*A silver cup that belonged to William Bradford, long-time governor of Plymouth and a major figure in the settlement.*

the city of Providence. Here other settlers gathered, many of them religious dissidents. Under Williams's influence the little settlement quickly decided that it would be governed by meetings of all the males, laying the foundations for a greater degree of democracy than existed virtually anywhere in the world. Inevitably these dissidents were an argumentative bunch, and throughout the colonial period there was much squabbling and splitting off of small groups to found little towns of their own.

But Roger Williams remained a powerful influence. He saw that these small, independent villages could easily be picked off one by one by neighboring colonies. In 1643, he went to England, where he got a patent joining several of the Rhode Island settlements into the Providence Plantations. In the preamble of the charter of the new colony it said, "the form of government in Providence Plantation is *Democratical*, that is to say, a government held by the free and voluntary consent of all, or the greater part of the free inhabitants." In time, Williams realized that his determination to pray only with those whom he believed were God's chosen people would ultimately have him praying alone. He did a complete reversal and established in Rhode Island the principle of freedom of religion for all. In the end, Roger Williams's influence strengthened American ideas and practices of liberty and equality.

Other dissidents would trouble the Massachusetts Bay Colony. One was Anne Hutchinson, who settled in Boston. Hutchinson was devoutly religious, but she had a strong and independent mind, and began to offer her own comments and opinions on religion. Her opinions attracted a lot of attention, and the leaders of the Bay Colony became extremely worried that she might challenge the religious basis on which it had been built. In the end they banished Hutchinson and some of her followers, who joined Roger Williams in Providence. Poor Anne Hutchinson eventually moved to Eastchester, outside of what is now New York City, where she and her family were massacred by Indians.

The Bay Colony's intolerance of different religious opinions appeared at its cruelest in the 1650s when some Quakers tried to preach their faith in New England. The Quakers believed that people found their way to Christ through an emotional or psychological feeling of being in contact with God. They found a welcome in Rhode Island, but when they went north to the Bay Colony they were sent away.

But they would not give up, and the Bay government, in desperation, passed a death sentence on Quakers. Three of them, determined to martyr themselves, came back to Massachusetts anyway. Two males were hanged. A woman, Mary Dyer, was on the scaffold, her face covered, when she was reprieved. Despite everything, she came back a year later, and this time they hanged her. "She hangs there like a flag," one observer wrote. Many people in Boston were shocked by the hanging of a woman, and the executions were stopped. Instead the Quakers, when caught, were whipped out of town.

All of this seems extremely cruel to modern sensibilities, and you might think that the Puritans, who had been oppressed for their beliefs back in England, would have more sympathy for religious dissidents. But they deeply and fervently believed that they were doing the work of God in building their city on a hill. It seemed clear to them that they had a *duty* to God to stamp out strange beliefs before they infected others. We must remember that many more religious dissidents were executed in Europe than ever were in the North American colonies.

# CHAPTER V

# Bible Commonwealths Spread Across New England

Despite the unceasing bickering over fine points of religion, the Massachusetts Bay Colony was a success almost from the start. It had intelligent, aggressive leaders, who had planned things carefully and who had seen to it that the settlers had what they needed in order to get off on the right foot. The proportion of the population that was literate has never again been attained in the United States, and the proportion of college-trained men was the greatest until the 1940s. They had the experience of earlier colonies to go by, especially the Virginia and Plymouth colonies. News of the success of the Bay Colony quickly got back to England. People there realized that the worst of the work had already been done, and they came flooding across the ocean.

Between 1630 and 1643, two hundred English ships brought twenty thousand people to Massachusetts, at a cost of what today would be millions of dollars in shipping and supplies. The vast movement of people to New England during the first half of the seventeenth century has been called by historians the Great Migration. In numbers it would be dwarfed by the waves of immigration of the nineteenth and twentieth centuries. But for the time it was astonishing: In those few years southern New

England was changed from a forestland dotted with Indian cornfields into a homeland for thousands of English settlers trying to create a miniature replica of England.

This large number of people could not be contained in the Massachusetts Bay area. Each family needed, or at least wanted, a substantial piece of land on which to grow corn, graze cattle and swine, and cut firewood. Little villages began to crop up north and south along the coast, and inland to the west. But even that was not enough. As early as 1634, only four years after Winthrop and his group had arrived, residents of the towns of Newtown, Dorchester, and Watertown began to see their areas becoming overcrowded. The soil was sandy and poor, too. They knew about the very fertile land to the west along the Connecticut River, where an epidemic had just wiped out nine hundred fifty of the thousand Indians living there. They decided to move out to the area in and around what is now Hartford, Connecticut.

The leaders of the Bay Colony, fearful of splitting the community into small pieces, would not let them go. But in fact there was no way they could stop such large groups of people from moving, and finally they gave in. So several congregations from the Bay Colony migrated to the Connecticut River Valley where Dutch and Plymouth colonists had already set up tiny trading posts. Here they drove their predecessors out and established a new colony consisting of the towns of Wethersfield, Windsor, and Hartford. It was a forewarning, for in time the lure of land would shatter Winthrop's godly city.

The creation of this new colony in what we now know as Connecticut had important consequences. The new group was led by an intelligent and forceful minister, Thomas Hooker. Hooker had somewhat different ideas from Winthrop's and the Bay Colony leaders' about how a colony ought to be run. He believed, for one thing, that church and state should be separated. We remember that in England, and in Europe generally, there was usually an official religion, which rulers insisted their people follow. This was also true in the American colonies: Virginians had to go to the Anglican Church and, as we have seen, the Bay Colonists drove away people who did not accept their religious laws.

Hooker, however, believed that civil officials ought not to have any say in what went on in the churches. That should be left to ministers and elected church elders. Not that religion would play no part in civil government. But the church and the government each must serve God in its own way. Indeed, many laws passed by the General Court in Connecticut, as in Massachusetts, were taken word for word from the Bible.

Further, according to Hooker, "The choice of public magistrates belongs unto the people, by God's allowance." That is to say, the people ought to elect their own leaders. Going even further, he insisted on the

principle that laws, not men, ought to rule. A governor or legislature could not on a whim order people to do this or that; they must go by the laws. And in order to see that this happened, a number of the principal first settlers drew up a paper called the Fundamental

*This is one of the famous beaver hats that were so important to the settlement of America. These hats were popular in Europe for many decades, and beaver fur was excellent for making the felt that went into them. Both Dutch and English settlers moving into Connecticut wanted to trade with Indians for beaver pelts. This hat belonged to Constance Hopkins, daughter of Master Stephen Hopkins, a* Mayflower *passenger.*

Orders for Connecticut, which spelled out how the new colony's government was to be organized. These Fundamental Orders, according to some historians, can be called the first-ever written constitution that actually set up a government. Even today Connecticut likes to call itself the Constitution State.

But the population explosion did not end with the new colony around Hartford. Other colonies were started at Saybrook at the mouth of the Connecticut River and at New Haven. Colonists were also spreading out from Massachusetts Bay into what would become the states of Maine and New Hampshire. The Bay Colony was thus the seedbed for the settlement of the whole coastal area of New England, as well as the area inland to the west.

*Josiah Winslow was the son of the famous Edward Winslow, one of the Pilgrim leaders. Josiah became governor of Connecticut and an important figure in his own right. Penelope Pelham, Josiah Winslow's wife, is on the right.*

*A typical lady of the mid-1600s at the time that the Massachusetts colonists were spreading into Connecticut, Maine, and elsewhere. She was Elizabeth Paddy Wensley.*

We should keep in mind that not all of these English immigrants were Puritans devoting their lives to God. Among them were indentured servants and a good many people who came out to New England simply to better themselves and get away from England, where the battling between king and parliament was brewing up to open warfare.

But to a surprising extent, the bulk of the people who came were indeed determined to help build the godly city on a hill that Winthrop had talked about. The colonies spreading out from Massachusetts have been called Bible commonwealths—clusters of towns and villages inhabited by people determined to live by God's laws. We cannot stress this enough. These were not casual Christians, as are so many people today. Their religion was bound deeply into their lives. They tried to make sure that everything they thought, felt, and did was directed toward one end: the glorification of God. And that meant, for one thing, keeping a sharp eye on their neighbors, for if anyone fell into sin, that could damn the whole community in the eyes of God and cause everyone to spend an eternity in hell.

For another, because early Protestants had a strong intellectual bent, they insisted that everybody be literate enough to read the Bible, and this was a time when the vast majority of the people in the world could neither read nor write. Furthermore, as early as 1636, when the Bay Colony was only six years old, plans were made to establish a college, and two years later Harvard was opened. The town it was built in was named Cambridge, in honor of the English university it was modeled on. The new college was supposed to train bright young men for the ministry and for leadership; but it was also supposed to provide an education that would serve young men in business and other occupations the colony needed.

Yet one more aspect of Puritanism was its lack of concern for getting rich, and most particularly an ardent opposition to any display of wealth. The point of life, for these people, was to glorify God through worship and service to mankind. They truly and deeply believed in their religion and tried hard to do their duty to God and man.

Unfortunately they sometimes carried their beliefs too far. The story of the hanging of the witches of Salem is one of the best-known events from Puritan times. In fact, it was not nearly as important as the legend makes it, but it was filled with drama and has been the subject of many stories. In the sixteenth and seventeenth centuries almost everybody in Europe and America believed in witches—people who, it was thought, were in league with Satan and had the power to fly around rooms, to make others sick, to cause cows to lose their milk, and so on. Witches were mentioned in the Bible, which was enough reason to believe in them; but many people claimed to have seen witches, or to have been harmed by them. Witches had been hung in Connecticut as early as 1647 and in Virginia as well. Witches were as real to people of those times as were God and the devil.

In 1692, some teenage girls in Salem began acting strangely and claimed that they were bewitched. This was a serious matter and was taken up by local judges. Unfortunately the judges permitted the use of "spectral evidence" in court—that is, they accepted as true what the victims of the witches claimed to have seen when being tormented by witches. Anyone could thus say anything about anyone else and have it accepted as evidence in court. Many of the victims began accusing various people around Salem of witchcraft. People were found guilty and were hanged. One man, a farmer called Giles Cory, refused to plead guilty, because if he maintained his innocence, his children could inherit his farm. He was crushed with rocks to force him to admit guilt, but all he would say was, "More weight," and he died.

Some of the Massachusetts leaders had been made uneasy by the whole thing right from the beginning, and within a few months they put a stop to the trials and released those still in prisons. Twenty people, however, had been executed as witches. As sad as the episode was for those who died and their families, we must remember that this one outburst was not typical of New England. Witchcraft scares were rare there in comparison to Europe, where thousands of people were burned or hanged for witchcraft.

# CHAPTER VI

# The Indians Go to War to Stop the Puritan Invasion

**W**e have been, in this volume, concentrating on the English set-tlers in New England, because much of what our country is today grew out of these colonies. But we must remember that the Puritans did not enter a vacant land. The region was inhabited by a lot of other people as well: the Indians. From the beginning the English had seen North America as a sparsely inhabited wilderness, a land almost empty of people. To the extent that some areas had been depopulated by the diseases that tore through Indian villages, this was true. Nonetheless, there were tens of thousands of Indians in New England, divided into a considerable number of tribes. Indeed, until about 1670—fifty years after the Pilgrims settled at Plymouth—there were probably more Indians than English in the area.

In truth, it would not have mattered very much to the English whether the land was empty or not. They firmly believed that theirs was a superi-or culture. Most people think their own ways and beliefs are better than those of other people and often use these ideas to justify exclusion and violence.

However the culture of the Indians was remarkably well adapted to the country they lived in. Until the devastation brought on by English diseases, the Indians on the Atlantic coast were a populous and successful group, living reasonably comfortable lives, despite occasional times of war or hunger. (For the story of the earliest encounters of Indians with Europeans, see *Clash of Cultures*, the first book of this series.)

But it was nonetheless true that the European culture of the English was technologically substantially more advanced than that of the Indians. The English had firearms, metal tools, ships capable of crossing thousands of miles of ocean; in addition they had a written language, mathematics, and much else. They were sure that the Indians would be impressed by these achievements and would quickly adopt English ways and the Christian religion. Soon, the English thought, the Indians would start building cottages and take to farming in the English style, and learn to read and write English and worship the Christian god.

But the Indians, like most peoples, were in no hurry to replace their ancient culture with a new one. True, they were eager to get hold of English weapons such as muskets and steel swords which they could use against rival tribes. They liked the glass beads, metal goods, and liquor the English offered in trade for beaver skins and corn. Some of them, seeing that the English were largely unaffected by the diseases that decimated the Indians, came to believe that the English god was more powerful than their own and converted to Christianity—or at least pretended to. But on the whole, the Indians had no desire to become English, and as the English continued to pour in throughout the 1630s and 1640s, their resentment of the intruders grew.

And with this we come to one of the great paradoxes of the English conquest of America. Had the Indians, at the start, joined together to prevent the Europeans from coming in, they could easily have done so. Despite the appalling death rate from epidemics of European diseases, the Indians far outnumbered the English settlers in the early days, and would continue to outnumber them for decades. True, English muskets gave the

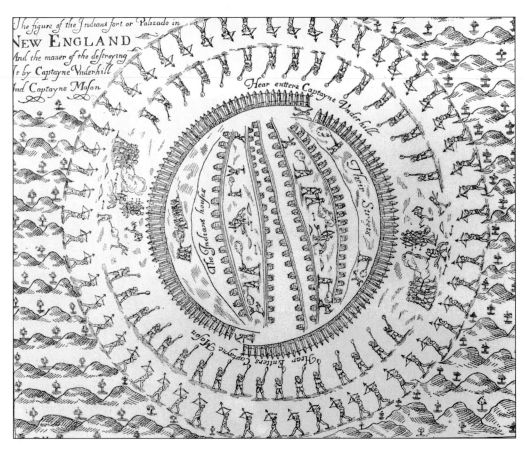

*This English artist's conception of the attack on the Pequot Village in 1636 appeared shortly after the battle. A circle of Indians with bows surrounds a circle of English with muskets. Inside the village Indians and English soldiers are fighting at close quarters.*

English some advantage, but Indian arrows were very effective, and early on they got muskets from the Dutch. There is no doubt that a well-planned attack could have driven the English into the sea.

The problem was that Indian groups—villages, tribes, alliances of tribes—were constantly in conflict with one another. This conflict did not inevitably result in warfare: The Indians were always making pacts and peace treaties among themselves as they maneuvered for advantage. But rivalries existed among them, and sometimes they were bitter. So instead of driving the English out, tribal chiefs tried to make alliances with the newcomers, in hopes of turning English muskets against the Indians' traditional enemies. We have seen how Chief Massasoit of the Pokanokets (Wampanoags) made a deal with the Pilgrims to bring them to his side in case he was attacked by other Indians, such as his enemies the Narragansett.

If Massasoit had decided in 1620 to run the Pilgrims out, he could have done so easily and massacred them in the process. This would certainly have discouraged other Puritans from coming, and the development of the English colonies in North America would have been slowed. But instead he offered peace.

At least one Indian chief, Miantonomi of the Narragansett tribe, saw what was happening, and in 1642 he tried to pull the Indians together against the flood of English. He said, "For so are we all Indians as the English are, and say brother to one another; so must we be one as they are, otherwise we shall all be gone shortly. . . ."

Indeed, Miantonomi knew from experience what he was talking about. A few years earlier he had joined with the English to destroy an Indian enemy, the powerful Pequot of Connecticut. The English were now quick to sense danger in Miantonomi's efforts to pull the Indians together. They did not want to attack him themselves, fearing that would trigger an Indian uprising against them, so they persuaded another Indian chief to kill him—yet one more blunder by the Indians.

Except for the brief but bloody Pequot war, however, relations between the Indians and the English settlers remained generally peaceful, if uneasy, throughout Massasoit's lifetime. (For an account of the Pequot war see *Clash of Cultures*, the first book of this series.) The Puritans still believed that the best way to deal with the Indians was to "civilize" them—that is, to convert them to Christianity and turn them into English farmers. A few of the Indians, with English aid and encouragement, created little English villages for themselves with Christian churches. These were known as praying towns. By the 1670s there were some four thousand Indians living in English areas, either in praying towns or actually mingling in English villages.

The old Indian culture was being eaten away. By 1670, the majority of Indians in eastern New England could not remember a time when the English were not there. Moreover, by now the English had begun to outnumber the Indians in the area, and more kept flooding in. On the eastern seaboard from New Hampshire down to Long Island Sound, the English were the dominant power though the Indians still ruled inland.

Some English leaders tried to respect the rights of the Indians, but

*Thatching a roof. The thatch is laid up in bundles in a carefully worked-out system that had been developed in northern Europe over centuries.*

*Keeping animals where they belonged was always a problem in the new colonies. This split-rail fencing was one type widely used. Note how the fence is set up in a zigzag pattern to give it more strength.*

there were many more, especially on the frontiers, who looked down on the Indians, cheated them at times, and sometimes dealt with them violently. The Indians were also capable of double-dealing, and over time resentments built up. Beyond anything else, the Indians could see perfectly well that the English were continuing to push deeper and deeper into land that had been home to the Indians for many generations.

But so long as Massasoit remained chief of the Pokanokets, an uneasy peace prevailed. When he died, he was succeeded by his elder son, who took the name Alexander, after the great Greek general. Alexander's younger brother, Metacomet, not to be outdone, took the name Philip, after the famous Macedonian king. (It was common for Indians to take new names on important occasions.) In 1671, Alexander died and Philip became chief.

King Philip, as he called himself, was an aggressive, proud man, who would walk the streets of Boston in splendid costume, followed by an entourage, every inch a king. One historian has called him "deceitful, vain and ambitious"; vain and ambitious he certainly was. More important, as a major chief, he felt he had a right and duty to do something about the English pushing their way into his lands. By the 1670s, he was having some success, as few before him had, in persuading other Indian groups to join him in driving the English out of New England.

His primary problem was the usual one: Old rivalries between Indian tribes were hard to put aside. The Mohegans, who had fought against their cousins in the Pequot war with the help of the Narragansett, again decided to side with the English to revenge themselves on Indian enemies. The Narragansett by now were no longer sure they wanted to support the English, and sat on the fence.

It was of critical importance to Philip to get his allies organized so that they could attack the English at several points all at once. Unfortunately for him, some of his Pokanokets jumped the gun and attacked the frontier settlement of Swansea, east of Providence, on June 20, 1675. Nobody was hurt, but some buildings were burned. The English were now alerted. The Nipmuck of central Massachusetts and other groups situated along the Connecticut River joined in, and by fall a real war between the Indians and the settlers was on.

The Indians had some important advantages. They were far better woodsmen than the English, able to slip quietly among the trees to mount surprise attacks. They had been fighting among themselves over this ground for generations, knew the land intimately, and understood where to set ambushes. By this time many of them had muskets, and knew how to use them.

The English advantage lay in their superior weapons, their boldness,

*Metacomet, the famous Indian chieftain and fighter known to the Europeans as King Philip. He liked to make a show and dressed in fancy garb like this when he walked through the towns of the English settlers. He died in the war named for him.*

and the fact that they outnumbered the Indians, at least along the seacoast. But they did not know how to fight in Indian fashion. Again and again the Indians lured English companies into traps, first appearing to retreat and then, when the English raced after them, storming in with a larger force.

At first things went the Indians' way. They would dash out of the woods into a settlement, especially along the frontier, burn villages and farms, and disappear. Seacoast towns like Boston filled up with refugees.

*A reenactment of a Pilgrim battle force. Note that long pikes were still part of military equipment. A force much like this one fought the Pequots.*

It did seem indeed that the Indians might actually be able to drive the English out.

But slowly, through bitter experience, the English learned how to fight the Indians. They needed Indian help, for the Indians had an amazing ability to see signs of humans in the woods. Indian scouts were invaluable in guiding the English to Indian hiding places among the trees and saving them from ambushes.

The question always was, which Indians could the English trust? One group they decided not to trust was the Narragansett of Rhode Island. After some attempts at making an alliance with them, the English mounted an attack. A Narragansett who had turned against his tribe guided a large English force of over a thousand men, including a number of Indians, to the Narragansett hiding place in the midst of a large swamp.

It was winter, and the English were able to cross the swamp on ice. Deep in the swamp they discovered a fortified village with a log palisade around it. They burst through a break in the palisade and fought the Indian warriors at close quarters while women and children huddled in their wigwams. Both sides fought desperately hand to hand, but the Indians were outnumbered. Their bodies began to pile up, and in the end only a handful of them escaped through gaps in the palisade. When the fighting was over, some five hundred Indians lay dead in the village. The English burned it to the ground.

It was a great victory for the English, for it dealt a heavy blow to one of the most powerful tribes in New England. Through the rest of the winter the English sought out Indian villages and burned them, destroying their food supplies. By the end of the winter many Indians were starving.

Particularly clever was Captain Benjamin Church, who had fought in the Great Swamp battle. Church put together a company of English volunteers with some Indians. Instead of traveling through the woods in a group as the English usually did, he spread his men out, making them less vulnerable to a surprise attack. Again and again Church's force beat the Indians. Finally, in August 1676, they caught King Philip in a trap and killed him. With the Indian leader gone, the war ground slowly to an end. By 1677, it was all over. The English had won. Never again would the Indians be a threat in New England. It was no longer shared land, but owned by the English, who could now do with it what they liked. More and more the English would deal with the Indians by reserving for them chunks of land. This policy of confining Indians to "reservations" became the basic one in North America.

# CHAPTER VII

# The Puritan Experiment Fails, But Leaves a Mighty Legacy

But if the conquest over the Indians was a military victory, it lay the groundwork for the end of the Puritan dream of building that godly city on a hill. It looked, at first, as if the dream would be made real. The original settlers did try hard to live righteously and to put the commands of God and the needs of the community ahead of the desires of the individual.

This was, needless to say, a very high ideal and hard to live up to. The first settlers had been driven by a great vision. They saw themselves as saints out to build a new world. But their children and grandchildren did not inevitably feel the same way. It is likely that the dream would have died anyway. But the immediate cause for the ebbing of the dream was something more practical: land.

Most of the earliest New England Villages had been organized on the dominant English pattern, with houses on small plots of land clustered around a church, perhaps a school, and a green or common where everybody's milk cows could graze. The land around the village was divided into sections, so much for each family to farm.

In these early New England towns this farmland was cut up in strips one hundred to one thousand feet wide. (A football field is one hundred sixty feet wide.) As the village grew, the strips leading away from the village out into the fields and forests grew longer and longer, frequently three miles long and sometimes six, even ten. People whose plots lay at the end of a strip might have an hour's walk out in the morning and another hour's walk home at night; and if they were taking a plodding ox with a cart over the deeply rutted and pitted dirt roads, it could take much longer. Inevitably, many people decided it would be easier to make their homes where their farmlands lay.

But there was more to it than mere practicality. In the England the settlers had come from, most of the land was already owned, or at least controlled, by someone, in many cases rich noblemen or even the king. Possession of even a small amount of land gave people substantial advantages over others. These English men and women came to New England carrying with them a mystique about land, a belief that ownership of a large chunk of land would raise them up. In addition to giving status, land was valuable for its own sake, of course. It was the source of food and clothing and gave independence from landlords. Beyond that, these Puritans had large families, and fathers had to provide farms for all their sons, and they for theirs down through several generations. From their perspective they needed hundreds of acres just to take care of their families' needs over the long haul.

And out there, after the defeat of the Indians, lay millions of acres for the taking—or so it seemed.

But the town fathers resisted. It was hard enough to keep people to the old ideals when they lived in the village, where the town fathers could keep an eye on them; if they were scattered across the countryside, there was no telling what might happen. The leaders' plan was that as the population grew, they would spin off new villages on the old model. Town meetings passed laws making it difficult for people to build isolated houses on their outlying farms.

*By the middle of the 1600s, the English settlers in New England were well established. This house, just north of the original Plymouth Plantation was built in Duxbury in 1653 by John Alden, third son of the famous lovers Priscilla Mullins and John Alden. Roofs were no longer thatched, but shingled, and shingles were also used for the sides. The house has been restored.*

But these laws were hard to enforce, and in any case, as time went on, people who wanted to settle outside of the villages gained a lot of votes. In the end the pressure on the town fathers was too great for them to resist, and there began to develop little clutches of farmhouses in outlying areas. Soon enough these people tired of walking two or more hours each way to church and demanded their own churches. Once they got their own churches, they no longer wished to pay taxes to the old village. Step by step, the village system fragmented, until the people were scattered fairly evenly across all of southern New England. The city on a hill had broken down, and with it went the old ideals. It was land that the new generations wanted, not stern morality. Roger Williams said sadly, "God land will be as great a God with us English as God gold was with the Spanish."

The important point here is that this process could not have happened while the Indians remained a force controlling the frontiers. Only when they had been conquered did land open up to allow this scattering of the population. Thus, it was the conquest of the Indians, as much as anything, that led to the collapse of the Puritan vision. By the end of the 1600s, then, the old spirit was going, and ministers and leaders were complaining about the "great extravagance that people, and especially the ordinary sort, are fallen into, far beyond their circumstances, in their purchases, buildings, families, expenses, apparel, and generally in the whole way of living." So died the dream of the city on a hill.

And yet these Puritans—William Bradford, John Winthrop, Thomas Hooker, Roger Williams—built better than they knew. Many of the ideals that we still live by in America today—or try to live by, anyway—come down directly from the Puritans.

To start with, a lot of our political ideas descend from the Puritans. They believed that everybody was equal in the eyes of God; today we give that concept a secular twist by holding that all citizens are equal, all entitled to vote. The Puritans believed that the Bible put limits to what any government can do; this suggests that constitutions circumscribing governments could be written, as were the Fundamental Orders of Connecticut. From this idea descends our justly celebrated Bill of Rights, which puts limits on the government's authority to interfere in our free-

Mafukkenukeeg
# MATCHESEAENVOG
WEQUETOOG *kah* WUTTOOANATOOG
Uppevaonont CHRISTOH kah ne
# YEUYEU
## TEANUK

Wonk, ahche nunnukquodt miffinninnuh uk-
quohquenaount wutaiuskoianatamooonganoo.
Kah Kekerookaonk papaume WUSSITTUM-
WAE kefukodtum : kah papaume nawhutch
onkatogeh Wunnomwayeuongafh.

Nafhpe *INCREASE MATHER.*
Kukkootomwehteaenuh ut oomoeuwehkomong-
anit ut *Boftonut*, ut *New England.*

*Ecclef.* 12. 13. *Nootamuttuh pakodtittumoenk mamuffe ke-*
*ketookaonk,qufh God kah nanawehteaufh wutannooteamooongafh,*
*newutche yeu mamuffe wunnefeonk miffinninnuog.*

Act. 20. 21. *Noowauwohheunncau Jewfog kah Greekfog*
*aiuskoianntamowonk noggue en Godut; kah oonamptamowonk*
*noggue-kum Manitoomunonut Jefxs Chrift.*

Yeuth kukkookootomwehteaongafh qufhkinnu-
munafh en*Indiane* unnontoowaonganit nafhpe *S.D.*

*Boftonut*, Printuoop nafhpe *Bartholomew Green*,
kah *John Allen.* 1698.

By the mid-1600s, some Indians in New England were adopting English ways and the English religion. These so-called Praying Indians lived in small villages of their own in Massachusetts. This is the frontispiece of the first book to be translated into an Indian language. It is a collection of sermons by the famous preacher Increase Mather.

dom. The Puritans came to believe that the church government and civil government should be separated. We today believe in the separation of church and state. The Puritans had their system of independent church congregations, run by themselves. Our town meetings, still held in many places to vote on things like school budgets, descend directly from the congregational idea. Finally, some of the Calvinists, especially Roger Williams and others in Rhode Island, believed in freedom of conscience. We today are fervent in our insistence that anyone can worship as he or she likes—or not worship at all. Of course the Puritans themselves would have been aghast at where we have taken some of their ideas; it was not the intention of the Puritans to create a country like the modern United States. Indeed, they hated democracy. But for better or worse, much of our credo grew out of their thinking despite what their intentions might have been.

Politically, then, we have drawn much from the Puritans. But we have also taken a lot from them in other ways. We remain a religious nation. The majority of Americans attend religious services regularly, and many of us take our religions quite seriously. IN GOD WE TRUST is printed on our bills, and we say "one nation, under God" in our Pledge of Allegiance.

Furthermore, we are a charitable people. Like the Puritans, we believe we must take care of the less fortunate among us. Unlike the Puritans, our laws do not require us to pay tithes to support our churches and ministers. Nevertheless we give enormous amounts of money every year to our churches and other charities as well, such as the United Way, the Red Cross, and many others, so much so that our mailboxes are constantly stuffed with appeals for money. This charitable spirit is encouraged by the United States government, which allows us to deduct gifts to causes from our taxes.

Like the Puritans, we believe in working hard. Our Calvinist antecedents worked hard in order not to waste God's time: To loaf was sinful. Today we are more likely to say we work hard in order "to get ahead." However we think of it, we believe in the value of work for its own sake. Even people with plenty of money feel that they should have occupations and often work very hard at the jobs they choose to do. Sons and daughters from very wealthy families, such as the Kennedys and the Rockefellers, get into politics or actually run the banks and investment companies they own. Americans don't respect people who don't work.

We have also inherited from the Puritans our belief in the importance of education. In most towns the cost of schools is the largest item in the budget. A far higher percentage of Americans go to college than in any other nation. Millions of older Americans, who already have their college degrees, take courses at night just to advance their educations. Another American characteristic is our idealism. The Puritans came to New England with the idea that they could build that city on a hill and change the world vastly for the better. We, too, believe that we can improve ourselves, our children, our towns and cities, our whole social system, if we only work at it. We do not simply accept our fate, but keep trying new things to see if we can make improvements.

Taken all together, it is clear that the city on a hill did not disappear altogether. Much of the Puritan legacy is with us today. True, many Americans, like the Puritans, are exclusivist, intolerant, and harbor feelings of superiority. But on balance, a great deal that is best about the American nation was handed down to us from those Puritans who struggled so hard to build a godly and charitable society.

# BIBLIOGRAPHY

**For Students**

Barden, Renardo. *The Discovery of America: Opposing Viewpoints.* San Diego: Greenhaven Press, 1989.

Calloway, Colin G. *Indians of the Northeast.* New York: Facts on File, 1991.

Hall-Quest, Olga. *Flames Over New England: The Story of King Philip's War, 1675–1676.* New York: Dutton, 1967.

Rich, Louise D. *King Philip's War, 1675–76: The New England Indians Fight the Colonists.* New York: Watts, 1972.

Sewell, Marcia. *The Pilgrims of Plimouth.* New York: Atheneum, 1986.

Wilbur, C. Keith. *The New England Indians.* Chester, Conn.: Globe Pequot Press, 1978.

For Teachers

Axtell, James. *The European and the Indian: Essays in the Ethnology of Colonial North America.* New York: Oxford University Press, 1981.

Bourne, Russell. *The Red King's Rebellion: Racial Politics in New England, 1675–1678.* New York: Atheneum, 1990.

Bremer, Francis. *The Puritan Experiment.* New York: St. Martin's Press, 1976.

Bridenburgh, Carl. *Vexed and Troubled Englishmen, 1590–1642.* New York: Oxford University Press, 1968.

Cronon, William. *Changes in the Land: Indians, Colonists and the Ecology of New England.* New York: Hill & Wang, 1983.

Demos, John P. *A Little Commonwealth: Family Life in Plymouth Colony.* New York: Oxford University Press, 1970.

Foster, Stephen. *Their Solitary Way: The Puritan Social Ethic in the First Century of Settlement in New England.* New Haven: Yale University Press, 1971.

Jennings, Francis. *The Invasion of America: Indians, Colonialism, and the Cant of Conquest.* Chapel Hill: University of North Carolina Press, 1975.

Kupperman, Karen O. *Settling with the Indians: The Meeting of English and Indian Cultures in America, 1580–1640.* Lanham, Md.: Rowman & Littlefield, 1980.

Leach, Douglas Edward. *Flintlock and Tomahawk: New England in King Philip's War.* New York: W. W. Norton, 1958.

Morgan, Edmund. *The Puritan Dilemma: The Story of John Winthrop.* New York: Little, Brown, 1958.

Morison, Samuel Eliot, ed. *William Bradford, Of Plymouth Plantation, 1620–1647*. New York: Knopf, 1953.

Slotkin, Richard, and James K. Folsom, eds. *So Dreadfull A Judgement: Puritan Responses to King Philip's War, 1676–1677*. Middletown, Conn.: Wesleyan University Press, 1978.

Trigger, Bruce G., ed. *Handbook of North American Indians*. Vol. 15: Northeast. Washington, D.C.: Smithsonian Institution, 1978.

# INDEX

Page numbers for illustrations are in **boldface**

Abraham, 18–19
Alden, John, 24, 25, 35, 82
Alexander (chief), 75, 76
Allerton, Isaac, 33
Amsterdam, Holland, 22
Anglican Church
    central authority for, 57
    creation of, 16, 17
    Pilgrims and, 25
    Puritans and, 52, 59
    Separatists and, 21, 23
    Virginia Colony and, 23, 25, 65
animals, 56, **75**
archbishop of Canterbury, 21–22, 57
Atlantic Ocean, 9, 39

beaver hats, **65**
Bible commonwealths, 27, 67–68
Bill of Rights, U.S., 83
Boston, Massachusetts, 35, 48, 61, 62, 76
Bradford, William, 21, 33, 34, 35, 60, 83
Brewster, William, 21, 22, 38

Calvin, John, 16, 36, **37**, 38
Calvinism, 16–19, 37, 59
    New England Calvinists, 20
    religious beliefs of Calvinists, 36, 38
Cambridge University (England), 21, 22, 38, 39, 41, 59
Cape Cod, Pilgrims at, 11, 25, 27
capitalism, 14
Caribbean settlements, 23
    slaves from, 12
Carver, John, 26, 33
Catholic Church, 15–17, 37, 57
charity, 85
Charles I, 36, 52
Charlestown, Massachusetts, 35, 48
charters, 51
    Massachusetts Bay charter, 53-54
    Providence Plantations (Rhode Island) charter, 61
children
    birth of first English child, 30
    early deaths, 15
    Separatists, 22
Church, Benjamin, 79

Church of England. *See* Anglican Church
church and state, separation of, 64, 65, 85
churches
    charities and, 85
    early church service, **40**
    Indian Christian, 74
    Puritans' establishment of, 56
"city on a hill" vision, 49, 62, 67, 80, 83
Coke, Sir Edward, 59
Conant, Roger, 39–40
congregationalism, 57–58, 60, 85
Connecticut, 64–65
    witches, 68
    New Haven, 66
Connecticut River, 64, 66, 76
Constitution, U.S., 52
constitutions circumscribing government,
    65, 66, 83
Cory, Giles, 69
Cotton, John, 35, 49
covenant theory, 57
Cranach, Lucas, 37

Dartmouth, England, 9
Declaration of Independence, U.S., 27
diseases
    Indians and European, 28–29, 64, 71
    scurvy, 10
dissidents, religious, 61, 62
Dorchester, Massachusetts, 64
Dotey, Edward, 25
Dudley, Thomas, 35, 49
Dyer, Mary, 62

East Anglia, 39, 41
education
    Harvard College, 68
    level of, 63
    literacy and the Bible, 68
    present-day Puritan belief in, 86

Puritans' attainment of, 39
Elizabeth I, 14, 15, 21
Endecott, John, 41–42, 49
England
    Bay Colony venture and London
        investors, 40–41
    civil war in, 20, 36
    during 1600s, 14, 20, 21
    during 1620s, 35–36
    English villages, 49–50
    Groton Manor, 41
    king of England, 14, 51–53
    land ownership, 81
    *Mayflower* voyage from, 9–11
    religion in, 14, 15–19
    Separatists' emigration from, 22–24
epidemics, 29, 64, 71
executions, 62, 69

farming
    corn, 28, 30, **31**, 33, 50
    in England, 49–50
    large-scale, **55**
    Massachusetts settlers' methods, 50
    New England farmland, 80–81
food
    dinner reenactment, **46**
    first Thanksgiving, 33–34
    shortage of, 10, 30
    Puritan dishes, **43**
    rolls and bread, **57**
    vegetable gardens, **54**
*Fortune* (ship), 34
freemen, 54–56
Fundamental Orders, 65–66, 83

Gloucester, Massachusetts, 39
government
    concept of limited government, 52
    convenants and, 27, 52, 56–57

congregational principle, 57
Fundamental Orders (Connecticut), 65–66, 83
House of Burgesses (Virginia), 13, 51
Massachusetts Bay charter, 53–54
Mayflower Compact, 25–26, 27
present-day political ideas, 83, 85
Providence Plantations (Rhode Island) charter, 61
self-government in America, 13, 54
separation of church and state, 64, 65, 85
Great Migration, 63–64

Hartford, Connecticut, 64, 65
Harvard College, 68
hats, beaver, **65**
Henry VIII, 16, 17
Hingham, Massachusetts, 35
historic parks, 13
Holbein, Hans, 37
Holland, 22, **24**, 36
Hooker, Thomas, 64, 65, 83
Hopkins, Constance, 65
House of Burgesses (Virginia), 13, 51
houses
    during mid-1600s, **82**
    early New England, **50**
    furnishings, 30, 58, 59, **60**
    thatching a roof, **74**
    typical homestead, **56**
Hudson River, 25
Hutchinson, Anne, 61

idealism, American, 86
indentured servants, 67
Indians, 27–**28**, 29
    agriculture of, 27, 28
    epidemics, 29, 64, 71
    at first Thanksgiving, 33–34
    Indian naming custom, 75–76
    Pilgrims and the, 11, 27–34, **53**

and the Puritan invasion, 70–79
    reservations, 79

James I, 23, 52
Jamestown park, 13
Jamestown settlement, 11–**12**, 15, 23, 36

land ownership, 51, 60, 79, 80
Laud, William, 36
Leister, Edward, 25
Leyden Separatists, 22–24
Lincolnshire, England, 48
Locke, John, 27
Luther, Martin, 16, **37**

Maine, 66
Massachusetts Bay charter, 53–54
Massachusetts Bay Colony, 35
    colonists and English government, 52–53
    differences between Plymouth and, 38–39
    farming methods, 50
    Great Migration to, 63–64
    growth of, 64, 66–67
    Puritan arrival at, 48–49
    religious dissidence and intolerance in, 59, 61–62
Massachusetts Bay Company, 40–41
Massasoit (chief), 32, 33, 73, 75
Mather, Increase, 84
Mather, Richard, 49
*Mayflower* (ship)
    construction of, **18**
    sails to England, 33
    voyage of *Mayflower* Pilgrims, 9–11, 20–25
Mayflower Compact, 25–26, 27
Mayflower II, **10**
measles, 29
Metacomet (King Philip), 75, 76, **77**, 79
Miantonomi (chief), 73
Mohegan Indians, 76

Morton, Thomas, 36, 38, 41, 48
Mullins, Priscilla, 24–25, 35, 82

Narragansett Bay, Rhode Island, 35, 60
Narragansett Indians, 32, 73, 76, 78–79
New England
    birth of first English child in, 30
    decline of village system, 81–83
    early homes in, **50**
    early villages, **49**, 80
    Great Migration to, 63–64
    land ownership in, 81
    Massachusetts Bay Colony and
        development of, 35, 48
    Pilgrim arrival in, 13–14, **32**
    religious colony in, 41
    voyage of *Mayflower* Pilgrims and
        beginnings of, 9–11, 20–25
*New England Company for a Plantation in
    Massachusetts Bay, The*, 40
New Hampshire, 66, 74
Newtown, Massachusetts, 64
Nipmuck Indians, 76

parks, historic, 13
patents, 51, 61
Pequot war, **72**, 73, 76, 78
Philip, King (Metacomet), 75–76, **77**, 79
Pilgrims, *Mayflower*/Plymouth, 9, 14, 29
    differences between Puritans and, 38
    Indians and, 11, 27–34, **53**
    Mayflower Compact and, 27
    Pilgrim battle force reenactment, **78**
    relations between Puritans and, 48
    voyage of, 9–11, 20–25
plague, 29
Plimoth Plantation, 13
    dinner reenactment, **46**
    Puritan dishes, **43**
    reenactment of Indians, **28**
Plymouth Colony, 14

differences between Bay Colony and, 35,
    38–39
first Thanksgiving at, 33–34
government, 25–27
Pilgrim arrival at, 11
Puritans in, 59-60
relations between Bay Colony and, 48
Virginia Colony and, 25
Plymouth, England, 9
Plymouth Plantation, 11
Plymouth Rock, 11
Pocahontas, 11
Pokanokets Tribe (Wampanoags), 73, 75, 76
praying towns/praying Indians, 74, 84
Presbyterians, 57
Protestantism, 36, 37, 38
    early Protestants and the Bible, 68
    Protestant Calvinists, 16, 17, 20
Providence, Rhode Island, 60–61
Puritans
    and Anglican Church, 52, 59
    arrival at Bay Colony, 48–49
    beliefs and system of worship, 38,
        41–42, 58
    differences between Pilgrims and, 38–39
    establishment of churches, 56
    lack of concern for wealth, 68
    legacy, 80–86
    relations between Pilgrims and, 48

Quakers, 62

Raleigh, Sir Walter, **15**
Reformation, 37
religion, 13–19
    Bible commonwealths, 67–68
    covenant with God, 18–19
    founding of a religious society, 13–14
    freedom principle, 61, 85
    Indians' conversion to Christianity, 71,
        73, 84

praying towns/praying Indians, 74, 84
religious colony in New England, 41
religious dissidents, 61, 62
religious intolerance, 61-62
reservations, Indian, 79
Rhode Island, 60–61, 62, 78, 85
Roman Catholic Church, 15–17, 37, 57

Salem, Massachusetts, 40, 48
    witches of, 68–69
Samoset, 30–31
sampler, **58**
Saybrook, Connecticut, 66
Scrooby Separatist group, 21, 22
scurvy, 10
Separatists, 20–24, 59
Shawmut, Massachusetts, 48
slavery, 12
smallpox, 29
Smith, John, 11
Social Contract theory, 27
Southampton, England, 9
*Speedwell* (ship), 9
Squanto, 31, 32, 33
Standish, Laura, 58
Standish, Miles, 24, 25, 33, 35, 36, 58, 59
Sudbury, Massachusetts, 35
Swansea, 76

technology, 71
Thanksgiving, first, **33–34**
tobacco, 11–12, 25, 36
tools, Indian, **29**
treaty of peace, 32

Virginia Colony, 11–13

Anglican Church and the, 23, 25, 65
colonists and English government, 52
Leyden Separatists and the, 23
Pilgrims and the, 25, 36
self-government in, 13, 51
witches, 68
voting rights for freemen, 26, 54–56

Watertown, Massachusetts, 64
wealth, Puritan lack of concern for, 68
weapons, English, 71–72
Weathersfield, Connecticut, 64
Wensley, Elizabeth Paddy, **67**
Weston, Thomas, 23–24
White, John, 35, 39, 40–41, 43, 46
White, Peregrine, 30
Williams, Roger, 58–61, 83, 85
Williamsburg, Virginia, 13
Windsor, Connecticut, 64
Winslow, Edward, **26**, 33, 66
Winslow, Josiah and Penelope Pelham, **66**
Winthrop, John, 59, 64, 83
    "A Model of Christian Charity" speech,
        51
    arrival at Massachusetts Bay Colony,
        48–49
    "city on a hill" vision, 49, 52, 67, 80, 83
    early years of, 41–**42**, 43, 46–47
    and freemen' voting rights, 54–55
    and Massachusetts Bay charter, 53
    and Roger Williams, 60
witches, 68–69
women
    execution of Mary Dyer, 62
    household responsibilities, **54**
work ethic, Puritan, 85–86

JAMES LINCOLN COLLIER is the author of a number of books both for adults and for young people, including the social history *The Rise of Selfishness in America*. He is also noted for his biographies and historical studies in the field of jazz. Together with his brother, Christopher Collier, he has written a series of award-winning historical novels for children widely used in schools, including the Newbery Honor classic *My Brother Sam Is Dead*. A graduate of Hamilton College, he lives with his wife in New York City.

CHRISTOPHER COLLIER grew up in Fairfield County, Connecticut, and attended public schools there. He graduated from Clark University in Worcester, Massachusetts, and earned M.A. and Ph.D. degrees at Columbia University in New York City. After service in the Army and teaching in secondary schools for several years, Mr. Collier began teaching college in 1961. He is now Professor of History at the University of Connecticut and Connecticut State Historian. Mr. Collier has published many scholarly and popular books and articles about Connecticut and American history. With his brother, James, he is the author of nine historical novels for young adults, the best known of which is *My Brother Sam Is Dead*. He lives with his wife, Bonnie, a librarian, in Orange, Connecticut.